INSTANT
Credibility

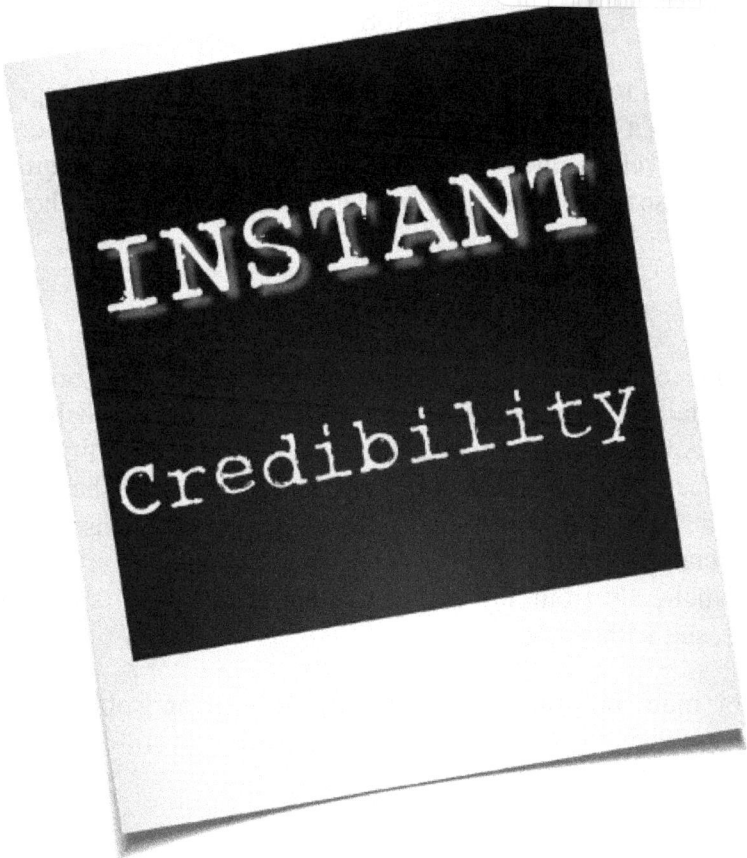

The 7 Step Breakthrough
Formula Transforming You
From Ordinary To Recognised
Industry Authority ... Instantly

www.InstantCredibility.com.au

ISBN 978-0-9875967-5-8

For more information on Amanda Robins or Robins Marketing please visit www.AmandaRobins.com

This Book is Full of KAPOW

"Amanda has truly delivered a kick-ass guide for anyone looking to get instant credibility in their business. I've been in business for 11 years now and have personally used almost all of these steps in my own business. I know they work. Just follow the formula Amanda gives you, and success can be yours too.

I can tell that Amanda put a lot of work and effort into this book. It's a fantastic read with tons of actionable information and entertaining stories. Plus she's co-authored with some fantastic experts I hold in high regard."

~ Monika Mundell www.MonikaMundell.com

I.N.S.T.A.N.T. Credibility is an excellent, well-written book by Amanda Robins

"I.N.S.T.A.N.T. Credibility is an excellent, well-written book by Amanda Robins. She has outlined in clear, easy to understand language how to use the leverage of a well written book to give you credibility not only in your industry or niche, but in your community and your peers. I would recommend this book to anyone who wants to give their business the edge."

~ Julie Lewin www.JulieLewin.com

Loved the exercises!

"Really valuable, complete advice here for people wanting to create a public profile quickly."

~ Natalie Kent www.SacredBusiness.com.au

I know Instant Credibility will serve me for years to come as I grow along with my business.

"I have read so many business books that have been helpful, but sometimes felt I had to plow through a lot of material to get to the point.

What I really appreciate about Instant Credibility is that it is a book, that contains all meat and no fluff. I like that the style is entertaining, direct and to the point with the natural steps to gain credibility no matter where you are in your business.

The stories and lessons from the different contributors add flavor and colorful real life scenarios to the lessons given.

I appreciate that the each chapter has an inquiry at the end and there is a free on-line diary available to keep track of your inner work.

This worked really well for me, who is already surrounded by too many notebooks!

There are also some other great generous bonuses given with the book to support your success.

I know Instant Credibility will serve me for years to come as I grow along with my business."

~ Beth Ann Fischberg www.YourMagneticPresence.com

Amanda is unarguably the Master in her field.

"WOW I.N.S.T.A.N.T Credibility is just that. It is not just a powerful, straight to the point book, it is an authentic one. It can only be described as a labour of love, a fastidiously researched, how to manifest I.N.S.T.A.N.T Credibility into your life. Fast and Simple, making it a wonderful reference especially if you do not know where to begin. Amanda is unarguably the Master in her field."

~Jackie Zenere www.SimpleGoodnessOnline.com.au

Do yourself a favor and follow her advice, I am!

"Having read numerous books and attended many seminars over the years Amanda Robins' book, I.N.S.T.A.N.T. Credibility was a refreshing change. Jam packed full of great ideas and step by step processes, Amanda is the go-to of AWESOMENESS. Do yourself a favor and follow her advice, I am!"

~ Sheila Kennedy www.SoundsFromSource.com

A MUST read no matter what your industry!

"Amanda Robins doesn't disappoint. Instant Credibility is packed with real world stories from experts who improved their credibility and propelled their businesses forward by following Amanda's 7 Step Formula.
Instant Credibility is not only a MUST read, it's a FUN read. AND it contains a ton of easy-to-implement exercises.
Thank you Amanda Robins for creating this great new resource!"

-Angela Tanger, www.WriteForHerHealth.com

Amanda has put her heart and soul into this highly entertaining and informative book.

"Amanda has put her heart and soul into this highly entertaining and informative book. She keeps the pace interesting and engaging with entertaining stories and quotes throughout! If you're wondering how you can stand out from the crowd and attract your ideal clients, I.N.S.T.A.N.T. Credibility will help you do just that."

~ Lisa Suling-Maslin www.LisaSulingMaslin.com

This book is a MUST for those seeking to establish themselves in business.

Instant Credibility is a one-stop credibility shop. Amanda has made a very very clear path for the novice and experienced to work through with concise and easy to follow exercises and chapters, fully supported by her highly regarded contributors. This book is a MUST for those seeking to establish themselves in business. I thoroughly enjoyed reading it and did so in one go, now to go back and do the work!

~ Heather Barker aka HeARTwork Heather
www.TheHeARTworkCentre.com

Just one of the easy 7 steps outlined by Amanda Robins will make you instantly credible!

Just one of the easy 7 steps outlined by Amanda Robins will make you instantly credible! Do all the exercises and it will elevate you to one of the experts in your Industry! It's a no-fail system backed by some of Australia's leading experts who share their experiences in Amanda's book INSTANT Credibility. Personally as I read it, I realised that I have been mentored by some of the best in their field in the world for business, financial and personal success but never thought to mention it in my bios, ever. That's Step 3 - Who has mentored me. Names like Ben Harvey who shares stages around the world with Dr John Demartini, Nik Halik for share trading strategies and also Gary Goldstein yes the Producer of 'Pretty Women' and other Hollywood Block Busters. My 'About ME ' page and media pack is getting a revamp!

- Terai Koronui - Love Life Transformation Coach, Author, Speaker. Author of 'SIZZLE - Be a HOT Date for a Perfect Mate'. Contributing Author to The Inspiration Bible -
www.TeraiKoronui.com

Dedication

This book is dedicated
to my husband Greg
and three boys,
Jordan, Jalen and
Terrell for always
supporting my dreams
and believing that
I can achieve
great things.

"Most of the important things in the world have been accomplished by people who have kept on trying when there seemed to be no hope at all."

~Dale Carnegie

InstantCredibility.com.au

Table of Contents

"Your worth consists
in what you are
and not in what
you have."

~Thomas A. Edison

Introduction

Thank you, thank you, thank you for taking the time to read this book. I know you have so many ways you could be spending your time and I am honored that you chose to trust me to show you how to boost your credibility.

The I.N.S.T.A.N.T. Credibility Formula ™ is a result of years of research, trial and error. It is exciting to be able to share these techniques with authentic business professionals like you.

While this book is full of powerful and effective ways to build your credibility, I don't want you to just take my word that they work.

I have hand selected 8 experts from a range of industries to tell their stories of the techniques they used to increase their credibility. Each of these experts are authentic and genuine people inspiring others and running ethical businesses.

Meet The Experts

Dale Beaumont is one of Australia's most successful young entrepreneurs. Having built three different million-dollar businesses before the age of thirty, today Dale is the founder and CEO of Business Blueprint®, the world's most forward-thinking business education company.

Dale is also the author and publisher of 16 best-selling books, which have collectively sold over a quarter of a million copies. Incredibly, 11 of those 16 books were published in a single year, a feat that earned him the title "Australia Most Prolific Author".

As a result of Dale's success, he has been interviewed on Sunrise, Today Show, Mornings with Kerri-Anne, Ten News, ABC Radio, Radio 2UE

Find out more www.BusinessBlueprint.com

Justin Herald has fast become one of the rising stars in the fields of business and personal development. At the age of 25 with only $50 to his name, Justin Herald set about changing the course of his life. Justin created Attitude Inc, a clothing brand that became an international licensing success that turned over millions per year.

Justin's success was so well noted that he was named the "INTERNATIONAL ENTREPRENEUR OF THE YEAR" for 2005. He recently was also awarded the Future Leaders Award, which recognises him as being one of the 50 most influential leaders of the next generation in Australia. In addition to the success of Attitude Gear®, Justin has produced his own products. Justin first released his business/motivational book in April 2003. Within 3 weeks, "Would you like Attitude with that?" hit the bestsellers list followed by Justin's much anticipated sequel, "So what are you waiting for?". He has gone on to write another 6 more best-selling books.

Find out more www.JustinHerald.com

Sue Papadoulis empowers entrepreneurs with all the skills necessary to get their own free publicity in the media.

Her students have appeared on most major TV programs such as Sunrise, The Project, Today Tonight, A Current Affair, Wake Up, Channel 7's Morning Show and Sky Business News.

Sue's goal in life is to inspire others to step up and play a bigger game by using the power of the media.

She is the celebrated co-author of two books – including the Amazon best-seller *"Align, Expand and Succeed"* and *"Ignite Your Business Mojo"*.

Find out more www.PublicityForProfit.com.au

Kat Heart is the author of "Home Business Queen" and the founder of Women's Web Marketing and also several Business Women's networks.

In 2009 after the birth of her daughter, her world literally falling apart, and Kat had to find a way to rebuild her life and her income. This is when Women's Web Marketing was born, along with an intense desire to share her story and teach Women why it's so crucial to have alternate income streams in place. "I am passionate about empowering and supporting Women with the skills, knowledge and mindset to grow their ultimate business... it's all about living life on **YOUR** own terms!"

Find out more www.KatHeartInc.com

Simone Eyles is the Co-founder of leading smart ordering company 365cups.com. The mobile ordering platform changing the way you order breakfast, lunch, coffee and tea!

Since 2011, my business focus has been 365cups.com, which combines my love of hot caffeinated beverages, technology and people. 365cups is a mobile food and beverage ordering platform, with a focus on coffee (of course!), that connects cafes and customers. Since going live, we have achieved the following outcomes:
• **WINNER Best App Food & Drink 2012 - 2013** Australian Mobile Awards
• **WINNER Excellence in Innovation** Murray-Riverina Business Awards - NSW Business Chamber • More than 45,000 app users • Over 150 clients across Australia and New Zealand
• Over $4M in revenue generated for our clients

Find out more www.365cups.com

Pauline Longdon is a professional copywriter and marketing strategist and author. In 2005, she was discharged from the Australian Army as a Major with Major Depression. Her brain was so messed up, she could barely read or write. She was told she was worthless and would be depressed for the rest of her life. But Pauline had other ideas. She began retraining her mind, studying belief-changing modalities and self funded her own rehabilitation. Her determination and investment in herself has accelerated her career in copywriting and marketing. In 2012 she became a paid copywriter and has since written for over 32 different industries. She has surprised industry veterans with her writing skills and ability to see through the clutter to find the "big idea."

Find out more www.TheCopyAlchemist.com

Con Dolmas helps online trainers find their authentic voice to create engaging training. Con Dolmas specializes in making voiceovers sound natural & engaging. His voice and delivery style have been described as: Friendly, Conversational & Believable, Caring & Empathetic, Knowledgeable, Informative & Authoritative.
Con is the author of "Voice Over for eLearning – The Essential Introduction for Online Trainers" and the corporate training narrator for multinational organisations including Microsoft, Vodafone, Telstra, Symantec, ANZ Bank, K-Mart & Novartis Pharmaceuticals.
Con has 15 years of professional business services (change management, business & financial analysis) across a diverse range of high-profile organisations, including QANTAS, Unisys, Optus, Vodafone and Kellogg's.

Find out more www.ConDolmas.com

Katrina Kavvalos is known as the 'Queen of Marketing and Branding'. She is a #1 Best Selling Author, Personal Branding & Social Media expert and trainer and **VIP Social Media Reporter for 'The Voice Australia', representing artist Will.i.am in 2014.**

Katrina has built high credibility in the Social Media and Online Marketing fields. Her high level of excellence, combined with her drive and zest for life, have contributed to her ranking in the top 1% in the world for influence and top 5% for the most viewed profile on LinkedIn.

Katrina is ranked in the top 100 in Sydney, Australia for most followed on Twitter and ranked in the top 50,000 most followed globally. A large number of celebrities, thought leaders and major brands follow Katrina.

Katrina helps celebrities, entrepreneurs, small business owners, speakers, coaches, authors and actors, learn how to grow their profile and super charge their personal brand, to become 'celebrities' within their industry.

Find out more www.KatrinaKavvalos.com

As you read through the pages of this book there is a lot of information to take in. To avoid being overwhelmed, take comfort in the knowledge that each of these techniques can be used on their own with great results and they can increase in power when combined. Take your time, enjoy the process and believe that what you are doing will yield results.

Now, let's begin your journey...

"If you are not learning while you're earning, you are cheating yourself out of the better portion of your compensation."

~ Napoleon Hill

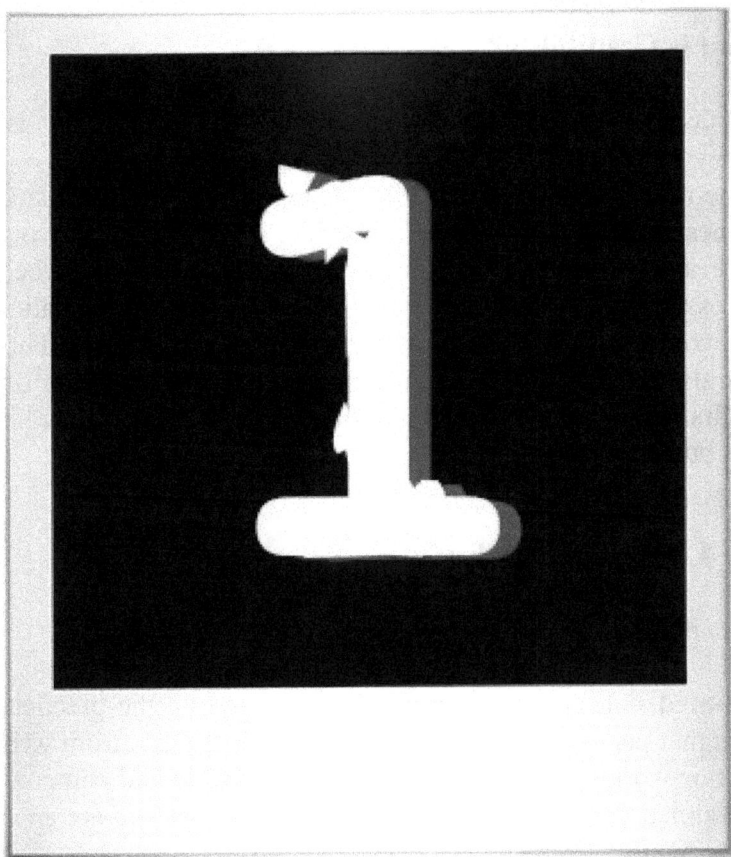

Chapter 1 ~
All about
Credibility

What is Credibility?

The Oxford dictionary states the definition of credibility is "the quality of being trusted and believed in."
In the marketing world it is well known that to build a successful business a client will need to know, like and trust you. Anyone can make a sale and sell the one product or service but to be truly successful in your business you need to build a solid relationship with your clients so they come back time and time again. This will naturally happen if you not only build credibility before you make the first sale but you back it up with every interaction you have in your business.

The 4 A's of Credibility

There are 4 Kinds of Credibility:

Assumed – This type of credibility is based on the preconceived ideas that people hold about you. You can get these from writing a book or working with or for well-known people and companies. It is assumed that because you wrote the book that you are an expert on the subject.

Appearance – First impressions count. If your marketing, website and appearance go against the image you are trying to convey as an expert, potential clients will see this. You only get one chance at a first impression and it is really important to make the most of it because it can take a long time to convince someone to work with you once they have formed a negative opinion about you.

Approved – This credibility comes from other people. If they approve of what you do and want to share that with the world through testimonials, referrals and endorsements, your credibility will soar.

Acquired – This credibility is built by working with someone and showing that you are the real deal. You have demonstrated your skills and expertise. While the other types of credibility will get your prospects to open the door, it is up to you to give them a reason to invite you through it. This is the part where many people fail. They have built credibility that is not based on a solid foundation of genuine expertise. While they made the first sale they do not have a strong community behind them wanting to continue to work with them, referring them to others and supporting them in future endeavors.

"If you've got to tell everyone how credible you are, you're not." ~ **Justin Herald**

Climbing the Credibility Staircase

Think of credibility as a way to stand out above the crowd.

Imagine that there is a staircase in which all business owners stand on in front of their potential clients. Now as the clients look up at the staircase trying to decide who to do business with, they notice that it is crowded at the bottom with people pushing each other trying to gain their attention.

As they look up the staircase, the business owners begin to thin out and at the top of the staircase are the real authorities. These are the people that inspire belief and trust. There is no pushing going on at the top because there is little to no competition and each person standing at the top has earned his or her place there.

That is where you want to be, at the top.

As you begin to implement the techniques you will learn in this book, you will take steps towards the top of the staircase. You will step out of the crowd of business owners begging for business and become the go to authority in your field with clients begging to do business with you.

The Trump Effect

Imagine earning $1.5 million per speech. This is what Donald Trump was paid in 2006 and 2007 when the Real Estate Wealth

Expo hosted by the Learning Annex hired him. While Donald Trump is very successful in his real estate career how much of this knowledge could he possibly share in an hour, which is how long each speech lasted.

It was not the information that Donald provided that he was handsomely paid for but it was because of his celebrity and brand he had created. He was paid millions because he was Donald Trump. This is what you want to create in your business.

The advantage of supercharging your credibility is that you can now charge the true value for your goods and services, which your clients are happy to pay for because they know and trust that the value you will give them in return will far exceed what they have paid you.

People are conditioned to pay high prices for expert advice. Think about it. If you went to your local GP and he or she charged you the fees of a Specialist would you be willing to pay that? Of course not. By the same token if you went to a Specialist and he or she charged you the fee of a GP, you would wonder what was wrong with them. Why is their fee so low? What is wrong with the service they provide that they do not charge Specialist rates?

Credibility lays the foundation for what you do so you do not have to waste time proving that you know what you are talking about, and can do the job better than you competitors. It paves the way for you to do what you do best and not have to prove yourself time and time again with every new client.

How to Use Your Power of Credibility for Good

Every marketing technique can be used for good but it can also be used to trick people. I want you to use the techniques in this book for good. You can build credibility with these techniques but they have to be based on real experience and expertise, or you will not only lose the credibility that you have built but any credibility and trust that you may have in the future.

People want to trust and believe you but if they feel that you have tried to pull the wool over their eyes they will be much less forgiving and with the power of social media today they will tell everyone they know about how you have treated them. There are many forums out there with bad reviews, which will last a lifetime, long after the problems may have been fixed.

"The rewards for building a solid authentic foundation of credibility will outweigh the profit you make from a sale based on trickery"
~ **Amanda Robins**

We Reap What We Sow

In the Far East there was an Emperor who was growing old. He knew it was time to pick a successor. Instead of choosing one of his children or assistants, the Emperor decided to find a worthy person to take over. He gathered all the young children throughout the kingdom to announce, "It is time for me to step down as Emperor. One of you here today will take my place".

The children were shocked and very excited at the thought of becoming an Emperor. The Emperor then continued to tell the children, "I am going to give each of you a special seed. Take it home, plant it and nurture it for the next year. Then on this day exactly one year from now you will all bring back your plants and I will judge them and select the new Emperor".

Amongst all the children was a boy named Ling. Like everyone else there that day Ling received a seed. When he came home from the palace he told his mother with excitement about what the Emperor had told them. His mother helped Ling find a pot and some soil to plant his new seed. Ling carefully watered his seed every day, watching to see what would grow. After about three weeks, Ling's seed had not grown at all. The other children began talking about how their seeds and plants were beginning to grow.

Ling kept watering and checking his plant as the weeks passed by. Still nothing. The other children's plants were growing each and every day. Ling felt like a failure. Six months passed and while other children had trees and tall plants, Ling's pot remained empty. While others bragged about how wonderful their plants were Ling remained quiet.

Finally a year passed and it was time for all the youth to return and bring their plants back to the Emperor for inspection. Looking at his empty pot Ling told his mother that he could not take it to the Emperor. His mother told him to be honest with the Emperor and take his pot anyway. Feeling sick to his stomach, Ling took his pot for inspection.

When Ling arrived at the palace, he was amazed at all the different types of plants the other children had grown. There were all different shapes, colours and sizes. Ling put his empty pot on the floor and the other children began to laugh at him. "Nice try", said one of the boys standing near Ling feeling sorry for him.

The Emperor arrived at the palace and he looked around the room. Ling tried to hide at the back out of the view of the Emperor. "Look at all the wonderful trees, flowers and plants you have grown children." He said. "Today one of you will become the next emperor!"

All of a sudden the Emperor spotted Ling trying to hide at the back of the room with his empty pot. The guards were ordered to bring Ling to the front of the room. Ling was terrified. *The Emperor knows I am a failure. Maybe he will have me killed*, he thought.

Once Ling reached the front of the room the Emperor asked for his name. "My name is Ling," he replied with his whole body shaking. The other children in the palace started to laugh at Ling standing there at the front of the room. The Emperor told the children to be silent. He looked at Ling, turned to the crowd and announced, "Behold your new Emperor, Ling!" In shock, Ling could not believe his ears. He thought there must have been a mistake after all he couldn't even grow his seed. The Emperor continued, "One year ago everyone here received a seed from me. You were told to plant it, water it, and bring it back to me in a year. What you did not know is that I gave you all boiled seeds, which would not grow. All of you brought back trees, plants and flowers but Ling was honest. When you saw your seed was not growing you swapped it for one that would. Only Ling had the courage and honesty to bring back a pot with my seed in it. Therefore Ling is your new Emperor!"

Exercise ~ Google Me
Google yourself ~ find out what others are saying about you. Hopefully it is all good. If you find nothing at all you have some work to do. If there is something bad you have a little extra work to do to overcome this.
"You can't fix what you don't know about".

Introduction to the I.N.S.T.A.N.T. Credibility Formula

The I.N.S.T.A.N.T Credibility Formula is a 7 step process to use what you have right now to boost your credibility, so the potential clients that you are attracting will recognise you as a leading authority in your industry.

Each technique is simple and easy to implement. On their own can be used for a boost but if you combine them the power magnifies.

As you implement each technique you will takes the steps up the staircase of credibility so you will soon be standing at the top above your competition.

The I.N.S.T.A.N.T Credibility Formula

Identity
Names
Social Proof
Teach
Author
Newsworthy
Team Up

Throughout this book there are exercises designed to not only reinforce what you have just learnt but to also get you started. So get a pen and a notebook to work through these when you come to them or to make it even easier, I have designed a companion eWorkbook to help you complete the exercises so they are all in the one place. This is a great optional extra.

You can get your free copy of the eWorkbook by visiting www.InstantCredibility.net

Have fun with what you are learning and know that if you reach the end of the book you are already in the top 5% of all people that will become a success!

Chapter 2 ~ Identity

The Key To Your Credibility

You are the key to your credibility. If you don't feel worthy to be known as the expert, your potential clients will pick up on that.

If you are not looking out for their best interests then they will pick up on that.

If you are hiding something and are not being congruent with the image you are putting out to the market place, they will know that too.

Many business owners feel the need to put on this facade of the professional that is always perfect and knows everything. That it can be a sign of weakness to say the words 'I don't know' or even admit to making mistakes. The fact is people like working with other human beings. What makes you human is exactly why they will want to work with you.

Everyone wants to relate to others. They want to feel like they belong and have something in common with the other people we share this earth with, so when they come across people that claim to know everything and to never have made a mistake in their life, these potential clients begin to feel inadequate.

I was at a workshop one day when a speaker took the stage. The very first thing he said was "I disagree with what the previous speaker has said. You don't need to have people like or trust you to buy from you". He went on to explain that there was a woman he came across that openly admitted to disliking him but she had bought something that he was selling. While I agree that they don't need to like you to buy something from you, I can guarantee that as soon as someone else comes along and offers a similar product or service as what you are offering, everyone will jump ship.

Business is more than just making a sale. It is about building a long lasting relationship with your clients so they will stick around for the long haul. It is about creating a community for them to belong to and feel like they are a part of your business. Without the clients and without the interest in what you do, there is no business.

Think back to a time when you have asked someone to help you and they answered your question by talking down to you as if you should have known that already. How did that make you feel? Would you be likely to ask this person for help again? Probably not if you could help it.

This is what many of the so called 'experts' do with their clients just because they think they show a sign of weakness by not knowing something, therefore they would not be seen as the expert anymore. This is far from the truth.

Every Success Story Is Also A Story Of Great Failure

Failure is the highway to success.

"If you want to succeed, double your failure rate."
~ **Tom Watson Sr.**

History is filled with stories of success but also of failure. Unlike the success stories, the stories of failure are not widely shared. Most people only get to see one side of the story so they believe that successful people are either lucky or just in the right place at the right time.

Can you guess who this is? This man failed in business at 21, was defeated in a legislative race at 22, failed again in business at 24, overcame his sweetheart's passing at 26, suffered a nervous breakdown at 27, lost a congressional race at 34, lost a senatorial race at age 45, failed in his effort to become vice president at 47, lost a senatorial race at the age of 49 and was then voted president of the United States of America at the age of 52.

This man who overcame great failures to reach the top of his profession was Abraham Lincoln. Even though he suffered years of failure, he succeeded in the end. Would you consider him a failure?

On December 10, 1903 a New York Times editorial questioned the Wright Brother's thinking. The thought of inventing a machine heavier than air, which would fly was completely absurd to most people. Just one week later the Wright Brothers took their famous first flight.

At age 65 with a beat up old car and a $100 Social Security cheque, Colonel Sanders knew he had to do something to improve his life. Remembering his mother's fried chicken recipe, he decided to start selling it. He knocked on door after door, some estimate over one thousand doors, before he finally sold his first order and look at KFC now.

A young cartoonist was rejected by many newspaper editors that told him he had no talent. One day the minister of a church hired him to draw some cartoons for him. While working out of a small mouse infested barn this man was inspired to create one of the world's best-known characters. This man was Walt Disney and that character was Mickey Mouse.

Successful people don't do great things; they only do small things in a great way.

"Our greatest weakness lies in giving up. The most certain way to succeed is always to try just one more time"
~Thomas A. Edison

Protect Your Reputation

Your reputation is one of the most valuable things you can own in your business. Equipment, staff and in some cases even yourself can be replaced but not your reputation. You can buy new equipment, hire new staff and even replace yourself or sell your business but once you lose your good reputation it can be almost impossible to get it back.

The joy of a good experience does not last as long as the bitterness of a bad one and with so much competition out there consumers have the power in their hands.

Many business owners leave it up to their clients and customers to decide on the reputation of the business and/or the business owners. This is not a good idea.

Your reputation is in your hands. You need to decide what you want to be known for, what qualities you bring to the table, and what others will be saying about you.

I can hear you now saying, "How can I make other people say good things about me? I can't control their minds".

While it is true, you can't control their minds but you can influence what they think and say about you.

Repetition is the key. If you want to be known for great customer service you have to keep promoting that. Not just say, "We have fantastic customer service". Back it up will real evidence that you are truly customer service experts.

You can also build trust in your clients and customers by following through on commitments. Under promising and over delivering far outweighs over promising and under delivering.

Many people fall into the trap of promising the potential clients the world to get their business and once they have it, completely letting the clients down.

This happened to me recently. I needed a couple of interviews transcribed for this book and I went to a site designed to help find freelancers to outsource work to. I listed my job and the bids started to come in. I decided on one freelancer whose price was really good and she said that she could have the work ready in 24 hours.

I funded the project and sent her the files. She agreed to the terms and everything was ready to go. So then I waited and waited. After 3 days I sent an email asking for an update. Then I went back to waiting. This went on for a few more days until I had had enough. I was so disappointed. This had put my work back over a week and now I had to find someone else. Luckily for me I contacted my second choice and she was very happy to help me.

Not only did my new freelancer stay true to her word but she also delivered my transcripts ahead of the promised date to a very high standard. I then recommended her to my network of business owners and left her a glowing review.

Holding true to your word will not only give you repeat business but it can also bring in business from places you never would have ever reached on your own.

What Do You Want To Be Known For?

Over a hundred years ago, a man picked up the newspaper and to his surprise and horror, he read his own obituary. The newspaper had reported the death of the wrong person. After the shock of reading about his own death had worn off he began to think about what they had said. The headline read "Dynamite King Dies" but it went on to say, "He was the merchant of death". You see, this man invented dynamite and after reading this he thought to himself, *is this how I will be remembered*? He decided that he wanted to leave a different legacy behind so he started to work towards peace.

This man was Alfred Nobel and today he is remembered for the famous Nobel Prize.

We all have a choice of what we want to be known for. Many people feel that if they narrow down what they do they will miss out on business but the truth is completely opposite. While you can offer many different things to your clients it is much easier to attract new business if you are known to be the best at something.

For example, if you were a web designer who specializes in helping accountants create professional websites, you will be first on the list of those potential clients rather than just another web designer doing a bit of this and a bit of that. It does not mean you are stuck doing this one area but it does mean that you are the go to person in that field. You are at the top on the staircase and no other web designer can compete with you without spending a lot of time trying to convince the new client they are right for the job.

Who Do You Work With?

Another factor to consider is what types of clients you work with. Many marketers refer to this as your "target market". This is where you list the age, gender, location, salary, interests and anything else along those lines, which can narrow down who you work with.

I on the other hand prefer to work with my 'Ideal Clients'.

Honestly I do not care about their age or gender, their location or marital status. Who am I to pass judgment on who will value and pay for my services based on how much money I think they make. People buy what they think is important. You can give the same amount of money to several different people and they will spend it in a number of different ways. They make choices depending on what their values are.

Don't Judge A Book By Its Cover!

A married couple stepped off a train in Boston, the wife was wearing a faded gingham dress and the husband was dressed in a homespun suit. They had come to see the President of Harvard University.

Upon arriving at the office of the president his secretary asked if they had an appointment. You could tell she was shocked that these backwoods, country hicks would come to Harvard let alone ask to see the president without an appointment.

"No we don't but we want to see the president", the husband said. "That is not possible", the secretary snapped, "He is busy all day".

"That's ok we'll wait", replied the wife. The couple sat there for hours while the secretary tried to ignore them. Finally wanting to get them out of the waiting room, the secretary went to the president to inform him there was a couple here to see him.

"Maybe if I give them a few minutes of my time they will leave", said the president and he went out to the waiting room to see them.

Upon meeting the couple in the waiting room, wanting to get them out as quickly as possible, he asked why they had come to see him.

The wife replied. "Our son had attended Harvard. Unfortunately he was killed in an accident about a year ago and we would like you, somewhere on your campus, to erect a memorial to him".

The president was shocked. "Madam, we can't put up statues for everyone that has attended Harvard and died", he said gruffly. "If we did, this place would look like a graveyard".

"No Sir", the wife replied. "We don't want you to erect a statue to our son. We thought we would give you a building that you could dedicate to him".

The president looked at the couple standing there in worn clothes, rolled his eyes and said, "A building. Do you have any idea how much a building costs? Harvard has over seven and a half million dollars worth of buildings".

The wife went silent for a while. The president was happy that now he could get them out of his office. The wife turned to her husband and said, "If that is all it costs to start a university, let's start our own". Her husband nodded and they left.

This couple was Mr. and Mrs. Leland Stanford. They walked out of the office and went back home to Palo Alto, California, where they established the Stanford University as a memorial to their son that Harvard no longer cared about.

You can never judge a book by its cover.

I used to run a beading business. I taught people how to make jewellery and I sold the beads and findings to create wonderful pieces of art. Now you would think that my clients would be female. Which most of them were but I had several young boys who came in each week to buy beads to make jewellery. A few of them came in with their dads. To look at them you would not think they would enjoy making jewellery but they loved it.

Have you ever had a client that may have fit your target market but their personality just rubbed you the wrong way? Let's face it, if you have to work don't you want to enjoy it?

I work with people based on certain personality traits. Here are the qualities I look for in my ideal clients.

I ONLY work with passionate, energetic and focused clients who are willing to learn and implement; clients that are on a mission to make a difference in the world and are willing to invest in themselves to do so.

Just imagine working with people who are suited to what you do. Who inspire you and implement what they learn. Who value your time and knowledge. Who are as happy to work with you, as you are with them.

Exercise ~ Work With Me

Make a list of the qualities your ideal clients have.

Who do you want to work with?

Who have you enjoyed working with in the past and why?

The Value Is In The Transformation

You are not selling what you think you are selling. People are not buying your widget they are buying what your widget does for them. People do not buy air-conditioning; they buy the feeling of relaxing in a cool house on a stinking hot summer's day. They are buying comfort.

It is the benefits of what you can do for them why they will buy from you, not the features of your offer.

Adding Personality

Have you ever had a time that someone's personality has clashed with yours or you meet someone for the very first time and you just clicked?

Everyone has come across people that they either have an instant connection with or are instantly repelled by. There are also relationships built over time once you get to know someone and your opinion of them may change. People prefer to work with people they like or find interesting.

Have you even looked for someone to help you with a problem and while they knew the answer they bored you to tears? I know I have and honestly I avoid asking them for help if I can find someone else that can answer my questions with a bit more personality.

Let's face it, personality can sell. Just look at some of the big brands built on a wacky personality. Look at Britney Spears for example. When she was having her breakdown and acting a little crazy, people could not get enough of her. Now she has settled down you don't really hear too much about her.

Think of an ad you have seen on TV. You know the ones where they grab your attention in a weird sort of way. They may be annoying or just plain silly but you remember them. You remember what they have said or what stunt they pulled to grab your attention. Now let me ask you. Do you remember that last ad which was the generic 'here is my shop, here is a slow pan of the shelves which are filled with the stuff I sell and here is a picture of one of my staff helping a customer'. No. Me either, but years later I remember an ad for computer security where the staff were all dancing around, then one person used the fishing line move to pull someone else into the dance.

The same technique is used in comic books. They have characters that have their own unique personalities. You will either like them or hate them. You can relate to some of their struggles and triumphs because even though they are over exaggerated there is a hint of real life drama that you can relate to. This is what you want to add to your marketing.

Just like I mentioned earlier, being open about your failures can not only help your clients relate to you it can also bring a sense of fascination about you that will make them want to continue to interact with you over the years, long after they have learnt everything from you. You are in business for the long haul and if you have a loyal following that really enjoy who you are, then your business will thrive.

On the same note if you are coming across as 'perfect' the interest in you, no matter how good you are at what you do, will fade. Take Superman for example. When they first published the comic book series he was invincible. He was a super man and nothing could hurt him. It was a new concept that had people reading intently but after a few issues it started to become boring. Honestly you knew what was going to happen. There was trouble and Superman came to the rescue so what they did was bring in Kryptonite. The one thing that can take away Superman's powers. All of a sudden he had a weakness. The plot thickened and people were interested how he would overcome this new obstacle. It is the same in your business. If all you are doing is promoting, 'Look at me. I am so wonderful,' It gets old quickly but if you show the ups and down in a strategic way, (beware not to over share. You do not need to tell them every little thing going on in your life) then you will keep the interest of your following.

"That is nothing like we thought it was going be." ~ Justin Herald

One of my favourite stories is when I spoke at the Tow Truck Drivers' Association's national conference. It was somewhere in North Queensland, I told some of my friends. They said "Oh that's going to be hard". I replied "No, that's exactly my market and I can just be me."

So I get there and as I don't get dressed up for anyone, I am dressed casual when I get to the hotel and the conference has already started. They were on a break and I was up next so I was just outside the room having a coffee, talking to a few guys. "How's the conference going?" I asked. They said, "Oh yeah, really good." I said, "What else is on for the rest of the day?" meaning what are they doing at the end of it all. And they go, "Oh we've got this wanker that's about to talk to us, some motivational guy, you know, he's probably going tell us how he died or how you know, we can do it and we stand up and pat each other on the back."

I said, "Ohh that would suck wouldn't it?" And they go, "Yeah." So they all went inside and then they introduced me and these two guys are sitting up the back mouths wide open going, "Oh crap, that's you."

And I said, "Look apparently I'm going tell you how I died, then I'm going to get you to stand up and pat each other on the back, but that's not what I do." And when I finished, they both come up and said, "That is nothing like we thought it was going be."

And I think that's where straightaway I had credibility when I walked up, but you've got to then back that up with your content.

Credibility is just a gift with purchase when you speak on stage. I don't take speaking lightly, I don't take writing books lightly either because what you've got the ability to do is to shape or change someone's outcomes or perceptions from what you say so that's why I deliberately do not do any multi-speaker events now because I was seeing what people have been taught was a whole heap of bull and

40

I'm not going to participate in even being there because it's all smoke and mirrors.

These whole 'get rich' conferences, the only person getting rich is the guy putting it on that is why at the last one I was a speaker at, I thought, *you know what, I've had enough.* I was outside, I'd finished speaking. I was the first speaker and then there was two more days of it. There was a lady outside with me and she says, "I don't know what I'm going do," and I replied, "Well, what do you mean?"

She goes, "Well there's so many speakers I don't know whose product I'm going to buy." I said "Well you shouldn't have come here looking to buy anything number one. But what you need to do, because it's a two day event, when you go home tonight and do this to me as well, put every single person's name into Google and see what other people say about them, not what they say about themselves."

The next day she came up to me and says, "You know what I found" I said, "I know, I know what you're going say". She goes, "There's two speakers that are speaking on stage that are bankrupt."

"Yeah, I know that, I knew that before I even got here."

So this is where a lot of people fall short. Getting on stage is credible but there's got to be stuff behind it, there's got to be foundation, there's got to be some stuff that people can actually trust and it's tangible where people can go and look at it. So, I mean people make mistakes and I'm all for that but don't trade off false credibility.

I've written a book or I speak on stage. You know, it's who you are when no one's around, is where your character really comes into play so that's something that was taught to me and instilled in me from a kid, it's something that I'm very happy with, you won't find one negative thing about me and there's a gazillion things about me on the internet, not one.

And it's because I know that I'm not dodgy. So, I know some people who were close to me, who spend a fortune trying to get

Google to take off stuff that's true. All because it's affecting their credibility now.

So, I'd just rather do the right thing, it seems to be cheaper.

Credibility will also equal longevity. As much as you can build your credibility, you can lose it as well, in a heartbeat, and there's this whole stupid saying that any publicity is good publicity. No it's not. Bad publicity is bad publicity.

It's not a set and forget thing. The one thing as soon as you put yourself into the public eye, you've got to constantly ensure that you're congruent with what people's perception of you is. It's not what the reality is; people's perception of me is I am a Ratbag. A good Ratbag mind you. That's fantastic because it's exactly what I am. I'm glad I didn't have to become 'prim and proper'.

Justin Herald

Justin Herald has fast become one of the rising stars in the fields of business and personal development. At the age of 25 with only $50 to his name, Justin Herald set about changing the course of his life. Justin created Attitude Inc, a clothing brand that became an international licensing success that turned over millions per year.

Justin's success was so well noted that he was named the "INTERNATIONAL ENTREPRENEUR OF THE YEAR" for 2005. He recently was also awarded the Future Leaders Award, which recognises him as being one of the 50 most influential leaders of the next generation in Australia.

In addition to the success of Attitude Gear®, Justin has produced his own products. Justin first released his business/motivational book in April 2003. Within 3 weeks "Would you like Attitude with that?" hit the bestsellers list. Justin's much anticipated sequel, "So what are you waiting for?" was released in May 2004 with an overwhelming response. He has gone on to write another 6 more best-selling books.

Find out more http://www.justinherald.com

Another added advantage to using personality in your business and marketing is you go from being a generic business competing with everyone else, to pulling the switch and changing your business into an attraction magnet. You will then attract your ideal clients to you while repelling the ones you do not want to work with.

Exercise ~ Fascinate Me

Make a list of your personality traits that you want to add to your marketing.

What type of personality traits can you add to your marketing?

What is it about you that will attract people to your business?

Show Me What You've Got

One very important way to build your credibility is to show people that you know what you are talking about. There are a lot of fantastic marketers out there that can make it look like you are amazing but if you can't back that up once clients come through the door not only will they not want to work with you, but they will feel a sense of being tricked, which is never good for your long term credibility.

One way to demonstrate that you know what you are talking about is to teach people what you know. I will go into this in detail when we get to **Chapter 5 ~Teach** but for now let me give you a quick exercise that will help you to open your mind as to the type of knowledge that you use on a regular basis that you can leverage to increase your credibility to potential clients.

Expertly Confidence

Are you ready to be known as an expert?
Do you feel like an expert?
Do you have the confidence to step into the spotlight?

I remember the first time someone called me an expert. A few years back I had a business selling beads and teaching people how to make jewellery. One Sunday morning I was helping one of my customers at my market stall pick out some beads for the necklace she wanted to make. She asked, "You're the expert so which beads would you use?"

This question took me by surprise. Not because I couldn't answer her question but because she referred to me as an expert. I certainly didn't feel like and expert. It had only been 6 months since I started making jewellery and I was self-taught by trial and error with information I got on the internet. That is when I realized that it does not matter if you feel like the expert as long as the people you're helping feel that you are the expert.

Let's face it. There will always be someone that knows more than you do, someone who has more experience than you do, someone who you can learn from but you can be that person to someone else if you have the confidence to step into that role.

"The Great Expert Experiment" ~ Con Dolmas

Here's a little social experiment you can try on your own.

Find someone whom you consider to be an "expert" in what they do, maybe it's someone at work, perhaps it's one of your friends or family, and ask them a simple question:

Do you consider yourself an expert?

If they answer No, ask a quick follow up question: Who DO you consider to be an expert?

If they agree they are an expert, ask "Who else do you consider an expert?" and then go and ask THAT person if they consider themselves an expert.

You'll be amazed at the results.

In June 2014, Business Communication expert, Con Dolmas, conducted this experiment with a group of highly skilled technology experts working at a New York Stock Exchange-listed multinational corporation.

The team had recently completed a mammoth system implementation and were in the process of assisting hundreds of employees across the country to maximize the benefits of the new system.

In the eyes of the corporation CEO and senior leadership team, these people were system experts.

In the eyes of employees around the country who were reaping the benefits of the new system, these people were not only system experts, but they were the only experts they trusted to help them resolve their system issues.

So how do you think these highly-respected experts responded to the question, "Do you consider yourself an expert?"

Perhaps surprisingly, they all answered NO.

But here's where it gets interesting.

Each team member was then asked to nominate someone who they believed WAS an expert, and 80% of those surveyed nominated another member of the same team!

So in the eyes of their colleagues, their customers and their managers, these nominated individuals were considered experts. However, from their own perspective, they didn't feel confident enough to acknowledge their own expertise.

When they were presented with these results and asked why they didn't believe they were experts, they all responded in a similar way.

...because they each felt there was someone in the world who was "better than they were", and therefore THAT person was the expert, not them.

They each felt they couldn't possibly be "the expert" because there was someone in the world who they considered to be better than they were in this area of expertise.

So despite the overwhelming evidence suggesting each person surveyed was indeed an expert in their own right, they each felt that simply because someone else knew more about the subject than they did, or had more experience in this area than they did, then they couldn't possibly be "THE expert".

At the conclusion of the experiment, when they were ultimately presented with all the findings, every member of the team eventually acknowledged, yes, they too were an expert in their field of endeavour.

So why the change?

Simply stated, they now felt confident enough to wear the badge labelled "expert".

They didn't have to be "THE" Expert" just "AN" Expert.

By shifting their mindset to acknowledge their own skills, they started to feel confident enough to admit to themselves "Yes, I am an expert".

The shift started to occur when they acknowledged that simply because someone else may know more than they do about a subject area, that doesn't make them any less worthy of being an "expert".

So what does this all mean?

Simply stated, being a credible expert starts with having the confidence to acknowledge your own expertise.

So let me ask you a question...

Do YOU consider yourself an expert?

Con Dolmas helps online trainers find their authentic voice to create engaging training. Con Dolmas specializes in making voiceovers sound natural & engaging. His voice and delivery style have been described as: Friendly, Conversational & Believable Caring & Empathetic, Knowledgeable, Informative & Authoritative.

Con is the author of "Voice Over for eLearning – The Essential Introduction for Online Trainers" and the corporate training narrator for multinational organisations including Microsoft, Vodafone, Telstra, Symantec, ANZ Bank, K-Mart & Novartis Pharmaceuticals.

With 15 years of professional business services (change management, business & financial analysis) across a diverse range of high-profile organisations, including QANTAS, Unisys, Optus, Vodafone and Kellogg's, Con has a strong track record with copywriting, e-learning script writing, documentation & workshop facilitation.

Find out more http://ConDolmas.com

You also do not have to be the best to be the most well known expert in your field.

Let's take Dr Phil for example. While he has a Ph.D. in Psychology he no longer holds a valid license to practice psychology, but he gives out advice to millions of people around the world every year. He may not be the best person to help people but he is willing to step into the limelight and be the expert, earning an estimated annual salary of $70 million.

> **Exercise ~ Confident Me**
>
> Make a list of reasons why you are an expert in your industry (add all your achievements).
>
> Look through your client's eyes and see yourself as they do. Why do they feel that you are an expert?

Circle of Excellence Exercise

Here is a simple technique to bring a sense of confidence whenever you may need it. It is a NLP exercise called, "Circle of Excellence".

Step 1: Imagine a large circle on the floor in front of you. It must be large enough for you to walk into.

Step 2: Now you need to fill this circle with all the times you have felt confident. Think of a time you achieved something great. What feelings did it invoke in you? What colour are these feelings? Now in your mind's eye take these feelings and put them into the circle. Repeat this over and over again until your circle is overflowing. (Your circle could be glowing. I like to see it as a bright sparkling gold colour).

Step 3: Step into the circle and let all those emotions flow through your body. (I feel my body starting to glow, filled with bright shinny gold confidence).

Step 4: Take your circle with you everywhere you go. If you are presenting put your circle on the floor and step into it before you take the stage, if you are writing put the circle at your desk, or if you are just suffering from self doubt put your circle on the floor and step into it to fill your body with confidence.

Are you ready to rock it as an Authority in your Industry?

I have created a Quick 5 Questions Quiz where you will discover if you have the confidence in yourself and your business to stand out as an authority in your industry.

Simply visit www.AmandaRobins.com/RockItQuiz.

"Many of life's failures are people who did not realize how close they were to success when they gave up."

~Thomas A. Edison

InstantCredibility.com.au

Chapter 3 ~ Names

Leveraging Credibility

"The first method for estimating the intelligence of a ruler is to look at the men he has around him."
~ **Niccolo Machiavelli.**

Machiavelli teaches a valuable lesson: people will not only judge you on your own merits alone, but also on the merits of your associates. If you want to be seen as a credible person, align yourself with other credible people.

Credibility By Association

When you are associated with a name or brand that is well known you gain credibility from them. Whether it is good or bad credibility would depend on who you connect yourself with.

You can leverage celebrity, knowledge and expertise and/or simply get in front of a client base that you would not have been able to reach on your own.

For example when Donald Trump had a feud with the owner of the WWE, Vince McMahon. It was the battle of the billionaires, which ended in Vince McMahon getting his head shaved at Wrestling Mania 23. Through a series of promotional tactics Trump was able to put his brand in front of consumers outside of the business world he was normally in.

This technique also works when you may be expanding what you do.

The entertainment industry uses this technique a lot. Can you remember the last time you saw a movie preview or an ad for a new TV show where they said, "Brought to you by the creators of", followed by a big name movie or show? They know if you like the previous product made by these people you are more likely to give their new project a chance.

That is why when Pixar brings out a new movie you know exactly who made it. Most people will watch it simply because it is a Pixar movie. They automatically believe that it will be good.

Who Have You Worked For?

Building credibility within a business can be similar to getting a new job. Showing potential clients who you have worked for and the jobs you have done for those people is very important. The bigger the business you have worked for the bigger the credibility you will get.

So if for example let's say you have worked for Apple and Frank's Computer Repairs. Apple will give you a level of credibility well above the other employer even if all you did was work in the mailroom. People have heard of Apple and are impressed by what they can do. So to get your foot in the door go with the bigger brand.

Potential clients also want to know insider secrets so if you have worked for a company that they know of and think they can learn something from you that you have learnt in your previous work, this can be a factor in why they want to work with you.

Exercise ~ Employed Me

Make a list of well-known companies, businesses and people you have worked for.

Put together a collection of lessons and stories your have learnt from your past work experience.

Who Has Mentored You?

Sharing the names of the people who have mentored you can really help your credibility. If you have learnt from the best in the industry, that will give you a lot of credibility to start with.
Your potential clients will feel like they can get the knowledge of the experts at a lower price than if they have learnt from the experts themselves.

They may also respect the knowledge of your mentors but they may not like the way they teach. That comes back to the personality. If they dislike the personality of your mentors and you have the same expertise to help them, they will come to you and be very happy to pay you for it.

You also reduce their learning curve. Think about all the time you took learning to do what you do. All the hours and money you spent learning from your mentors. When potential clients come along they know they want the job done right the first time by someone who knows what they are doing. You can save them hundreds of hours and thousands of dollars by sharing the knowledge of the mentors you have learnt from. It can really help to launch your career if you are just starting out. Before you have a lot of happy clients you can leverage the credibility of those who have taught you.

Exercise ~ Mentor Me

Make a list of people who you have learnt from.

Put together a collection of lessons and stories you have learnt from your mentors that you can share in your business.

Building Rapport with the Game Changers ~ Pauline Longdon

In July 2012, I finally achieved a major goal of mine to become a paid professional copywriter (a person who writes marketing material to sell "off the page") I had been studying for a year or two previously, but I had no real luck at getting my foot in the door.

I thought it was because I lacked the talent or skills I needed. But from all reports, my writing skills were decent enough for my level of experience. What I was missing was the credibility and connection to people with credibility.

I found social media to be a great "leveler" of the playing field. It gave me unprecedented access to the people who had the credibility I was looking for.
I effortlessly connected with the "game changers" in the industry and started to build up rapport and eventually friendships with them. Now some of them are the closest friends I've had.

I have been mentored and coached by some of the best copywriter marketers I could get access to. People like Mal Emery, Pete Godfrey, Trevor "Toe Cracker" Crook, Alexi Neocleous, Bret Thomson, Ted Nicholas, Lorrie Morgan Fererro and a few others I am keeping to myself. These names may not mean much to you, however in my world... they are a big deal. They have made millions of dollars for themselves and their clients. They are solid role models and working with them has definitely increased my credibility.

None of this has come cheaply though, and on many occasions I have had to invest in myself beyond any level I thought possible or comfortable.

Here is a tip for people wanting to boost their credibility and profile quickly. Take photos... lots of them. We live in an age where we have more access to cameras than ever before. When you are standing next to these credible giants in the industry, have your photo taken with them. If you are at a conference... take your nametag off. This makes it look more professional and as though the encounter was on more equal footing. Instead of you looking like a desperate groupie.

And most important of all... post the photo's strategically on your social media. (Always be thinking strategically... nothing should happen by accident!)

A very important distinction is... you need to be 100% authentic. You cannot be fake and expect to get far in any industry. The people I have connected with are not fools and are immune to being manipulated by 'try hards'. Be respectful, honest, and honour them by being your authentic self.

People watching my accelerated career have often remarked on the incredible connection I have with the main players in the industry. Some of them shake their heads in disbelief when they hear about who knows me and who is talking about me.

When I was in the Army, we had a saying "It's not what you know, it's who you know." I have a new saying "It's not about who you know... it's about who knows you!"

Pauline Longdon is a professional copywriter and marketing strategist and author. In 2005, she was discharged from the Australian Army as a Major with Major Depression. Her brain was so messed up, she could barely read or write. She was told she was worthless and would be depressed for the rest of her life. But Pauline had other ideas. She began retraining her mind, studying belief-changing modalities and self funded her own rehabilitation. Her determination and investment in herself has accelerated her career in copywriting and marketing. In 2012 she became a paid copywriter and has since written for over 32 different industries. She has surprised industry veterans with her writing skills and ability to see through the clutter to find the "big idea."
Pauline's skills are in high demand both in Australia and overseas.

Find out more http://thecopyalchemist.com

What Stories Of Successful People Can You Share?

Sharing the stories of well-known people can help build your credibility. Some people have built a career talking about others.

Let's take Napoleon Hill for example. This is a man that wrote what is considered to be the business bible for all entrepreneurs.

Napoleon Hill was asked one day by a man named Andrew Carnegie to study the characteristics of a large number of men who had achieved great wealth during their life time. Through years of research Hill discovered the 16 'laws' of success in which he wrote about 13 of these in his book, "Think and Grow Rich".

One of the things that gave Hill credibility was the men he interviewed to discover these principles. They included Henry Ford, William Wrigley Jr., John Wanamaker, James J. Hill, George S. Parker, E. M. Statler, Henry L. Doherty, Cyrus H. K. Curtis, George Eastman, Theodore Roosevelt, John W. Davis, Elbert Hubbard, Wilbur Wright, William Jennings, John D. Rockefeller, Charles M. Schwab, Thomas A. Edison and many, many more.

By leveraging the names, knowledge and the stories of these great men "Think and Grow Rich" has sold over 70 million copies and Napoleon Hill is a well-known author.

Using stories about successful people can help you to relate to your potential clients by giving them someone to relate to that they already know.

A great way people do this is by sharing stories of success by people who have done extraordinary things especially if they have overcome failure to do so.

Here is an example of some well-known people who overcome the odds to create success.

Above All Odds

"Your son is too stupid to learn, get him out of school" is what the note read that Tommy handed to his mother. His teacher had wrote it and sent it home with the 4yr old partially deaf child.

"My Tommy is not stupid," his mother said, "I will teach you myself". And that she did. Little Tommy grew up to be the great Thomas Edison. Partially deaf and with only 3 months of formal schooling he is one of the great inventors of all time.

In the first car he ever made, Henry Ford forgot to put in a reverse gear. That would have created some problems.

Would you consider these men to be failures?

Not at all. They succeeded in spite of the problems they faced not the absence of them.

This is called failing forward. No matter how many times they faced a setback, they learnt from it and kept moving forward to find the solution. It is not about luck like it appears to the outside world.

Thomas Edison failed approximately 10,000 times while he was working on the light bulb. Henry Ford was broke at the age of 40 and a Young Beethoven was told that he had no talent, but he gave some of the best music to the world.

All of these men beat the odds to become successful and you can too.

"Just because something doesn't do what you planned it to do doesn't mean it's useless"
~Thomas A. Edison

Who Can You Be Compared To?

Who are you similar to? What can you do that other industry leaders do? Could you be the Michael Jordan of business coaching?

You often hear news stories comparing people. My husband watches a lot of sporting news stories and you quite often hear them comparing today's players to the greats of the past. Whether it is their playing styles or their accomplishments, once they are in the same league as the greats then their credibility and value as a player rises.

You can do the same thing. You could be the Oprah of Australian television or the Donald Trump of Internet Marketing.

Who Can You Been Seen With?

Sharing the stage, taking a picture, teaching at the same event and even just having your book on the shelf next to a well-known author can bring you credibility.

Exercise ~ See Me

Collect pictures of well-known people you have been seen with.

Make a list of well-known people you want to be seen with. Put it out in the universe and see what opportunities arise for you.

Shameless Name Dropping

While it can boost your credibility to be associated with well-known people and brands, you can take it a step too far. If all you are doing is shamelessly dropping names (telling people all the time who you have worked with to impress them) then you will actually hurt your credibility. While they will find it fascinating who you have worked for, with or been mentored by, if all you have to show is some big names they will view you as a fraud with no substance. The best way to use these techniques is to just mention them in passing like it is not big deal. Add a story to your blog posts to show an example of what you are talking about. Put the pictures you may have on your website in places where people will notice but not make a big feature of them.

Be subtle when using these methods. You know what you are trying to achieve and you will do that bit by bit without having to shove it in people's faces.

Chapter 4 ~ Social Proof

Getting Others To Sell For You

The power of a recommendation can outweigh any other parts of your marketing. You see if you are telling everyone how wonderful you are, they may feel you have a hidden agenda and maybe you are a little full of yourself, but if someone else says that you are great they are more likely to believe it even if it comes from a complete stranger.

How many times have you seen a new product and thought about getting it but you were unsure? Then one of your friend's bought the product and loved it so you went out and got one for yourself.

Many people want to know if the product or service lives up to the promotional hype. They may have been ripped off and disappointed in the past so they are looking to be reassured that they are making a good decision.

They may want to buy what you have and need a little convincing that they are making the right decision. This is where social proof comes in.

The E.N.D.O.R.S.E Social Proof System

Throughout history there has always been a battle for consumer attention. Luckily we live in an age where social proof can be easily used and shared around the world at the speed of light. The system that I am about to show you, reveals the different types of social proof you can use to build your credibility and attract quality clients.

Expert
Numbers
Demonstration
Our Friends
Relationship
Superstar
End User

Expert

This type of social proof comes from a credible expert in your industry. This can also come through magazines and bloggers who are regarded as the go to expert on the subject.

Having a testimonial from a highly regarded expert in your field can really boost how potential clients see you. If they respect the person giving the testimonial and view them as an expert, then this person is saying that you are incredible and it must be true.

Numbers

Crowds have power. People feel safe in the knowledge that others before them have tried and tested products and services, so that has taken the risk away from them. Take McDonalds for example. In 1955 Ray Kroc started using 'Over 1 Million Served' in his advertising. Now, 1 million people can't be wrong.

Take apps for example. How many times have you looked at the number of downloads an app has when you go to download it from the app store? Has it helped to make the decision to get that app? If the app has only been downloaded 1 hundred times in 6 months, you may begin to wonder what was wrong with it, but if it had been downloaded over 1 million times then you think there has to be something you are missing out on.

This also applies to the New York Time Bestseller List. If a book has sold enough copies to be on that list then people assume it must be a good book.

Demonstration

Have you ever been in the supermarket and an announcement came over the loud speaker that there will be a free demonstration starting shortly? I have. I remember doing the weekly shopping and they announced you could get a free knife by watching a demonstration. There was a lady demonstrating a knife set. She showed people how sharp they were, how they could cut through a number of different things and how they didn't need sharpening even after they cut through things like a tin can. I would have to say I was impressed as were the other people watching. It was amazing to see the people rush to the front to get a set of these knives.

That is the power of showing people how your product or service works. It takes away the doubt and shows that you are not just full of words, you can back it up.

Our Friends

We all listen to our friends whether they are complaining or praising something. We know them and trust them so if they tell you something is great then you believe it usually with no questions asked. This is why you often find the 'Invite Friends' built into many marketing campaigns.

Take Zynga's games for example. Every so often it will pop up on your screen to invite your friends to play with you. It can be done as a social thing but you can also be rewarded for the number of friends you invite. They even cap the number of lives you have available to use and when you run out you simply ask your friends to send you more. By simply getting people to invite their friends to play, Zynga grew from 3 million daily users to 41 million average users in 2008 to 2009.

Relationship

One of the biggest things you can do with people is build a relationship with them. This takes time but it can be one of the most rewarding things any business owner can do. Once you have created a relationship filled with trust, you then have a platform that will enable you to bring out new products and services that will be embraced by your loyal clients. To build this relationship you need to interact with them. Using social media to show your personality and knowledge like we have previously discussed is an amazing way to build a strong long lasting relationship with your client base.

Superstar

A celebrity endorsement can be an incredible springboard to launch your product or service. If a celebrity is seen using your product or simply tweets about it, your sales can go through the roof. This is why big companies give away their products to celebrities in gift bags at award nights. The cost of giving away diamond watches to the superstars compared to how much money they make selling these watches to everyday people who want to be just like the celebrity is nothing (and far less than it would cost to pay them to be a spokesperson for your brand).

Take 'Beats by Dre' Headphones for example, they are now a fashion accessory for many celebrities. Who would have thought big chucky headphones worn around your neck would be a fashion statement but yet it is the in thing to do. It is increasingly popular by athletes to wear these on their way to their events. These headphones cost hundreds of dollars but because they are what all the celebrities are wearing that is what teenagers want to wear too. In 2014 Apple reportedly acquired Beats Electronics – The Company that makes 'Beats by Dre', for US$3 Billion. That is not a bad payday.

End User

Reviews can either help or hurt your business. Websites such as Yelp.com allow people to post reviews on the products and services they have used. It is fast becoming a habit for people to look at sites like these before trying something new. For example if you were thinking about trying out a new restaurant in town but are not quite sure on the quality of the food or the customer experience you will have, you would visit one of these sites and read the reviews. If they were good then chances are you would try the restaurant but if they were negative reviews then you would opt for a different restaurant.

eBay is a good example of this. I know personally before I buy anything from a seller that I have not heard of before I read the feedback previous buyers have left. I also do this when the product I am about to buy seems a little too cheap. I look to see if other people have purchased this exact product and if they were happy with the quality that was provided.

Ways To Use Social Proof

Now you know all the different types of social proof here are some ways that you can use them in your marketing.

Before and After Pictures

The weight loss industry is built on these. The before and after shoots are a very simple but very effective way to show the transformation you provide.

Other examples can include before and after pictures of renovations, skin care results, lawn care and makeovers, just to name a few.

Testimonials

A testimonial is great if it is done in a certain way. Anyone can have a testimonial saying, "John Smith is fantastic" but no one really cares about that. They want the proof. They want to see how you have improved someone else's life.

Case Studies

Think of a case study like a story. It is a story of how someone had a problem and took steps to overcome that problem to achieve the results they wanted, or better.

Now the case study does not have to be directly related to what you have done. It does not need to be your story or the story of one of your clients. It can be the story of how someone used similar techniques to those that you use and how they have achieved great results using them. This is very helpful for people that are just starting out. You know the techniques work but you have not had the time to test or use them all yourself, so you find others that have used these techniques and ask to use their stories as case studies to prove your point.

"Often Underestimated But It Is Something That You Cannot Put A Price On" ~ Dale Beaumont

To increase your profile and also, in turn, your credibility you should have third party endorsements or testimonials. It can be extremely powerful when others can provide you with written, audio or video testimonials – it is often underestimated but it is something that you cannot put a price on.

Think about when you often see an advert for a movie that is being released. They show you the trailer but also viewers walking out of the cinema that have just watched it, and they comment on what they thought about it. You have no idea who that person is, but because they are removed from the project, meaning they are not the director, producer or actor, we believe what they have to say because they don't have a vested interest. Of course the people who made the film are going to say it is fantastic, but if strangers also think that, then we are much more likely to go and see it.

There is a simple rule to follow when it comes to collecting endorsements – as long as the person giving it is not you, then you are off to a good start. It can be better and more powerful if the person giving the testimonial is well-known in your industry, however, a stranger is also really beneficial.

Once you have collected some of these testimonials, my advice to you is to start putting them everywhere. This includes on your website, in all of your marketing material, and throughout your presentations. You could even go as far as to print one onto a postcard and send it out to potential leads and clients. Alternatively if you are an employee, you can add them to your resume.

I heard a story about a person who was going for a major contract with a really large corporation. To stand out from the competition, they sent over a box which contained over 1000 written pages of testimonials from previous clients. I don't imagine that the company would have read all of them, however, that box which would have weighed over 10kgs certainly made a statement.

Now I'd like to give you the formula for getting a testimonial from someone. What typically happens when someone is asked to give a testimonial is they will automatically say "Dale Beaumont was amazing, brilliant, great etc". However, that doesn't really describe anything about what I do or what I can provide for a potential customer. To make the testimonial more effective and powerful, you can follow this formula: "I once was lost and now I'm found."

For example, if someone can write a testimonial along the lines of: "Seven months ago, I knew nothing about the subject of book publishing. I really didn't know how to begin the process of writing my book; however, once I came across Dale Beaumont's product, my learning skyrocketed. I have now completed my book, self-published it and have already sold 1000 copies. I am so appreciative of Dale's knowledge and would recommend this product to anyone." Can you see the difference? This testimonial is much stronger and I can use it on all my marketing material from now on.

FIVE QUICK TAKEAWAYS

1. Great testimonials are priceless, they can work wonders for your profile.
2. It helps that the person giving you an endorsement has a profile themselves, but even if they are a stranger, as long as it is genuine it will still work.
3. Once you have collected the testimonials put them everywhere; your website, marketing material, throughout your presentations etc.
4. Remember the formula "I once was lost and now I'm found".
5. Make it a habit to gather a few new testimonials each month as it's good to keep things fresh.

Dale Beaumont is one of Australia's most successful young entrepreneurs. Having built three different million-dollar businesses before the age of thirty, today Dale is the founder and CEO of Business Blueprint®, the world's most forward-thinking business education company.
Dale is also the author and publisher of 16 best-selling books, which have collectively sold over a quarter of a million copies. Incredibly, 11 of those 16 books were published in a single year, a

feat that earned him the title "Australia Most Prolific Author".

As a result of Dale's success, he has been interviewed on Sunrise, Today Show, Mornings with Kerri-Anne, Ten News, ABC Radio, Radio 2UE as well as being featured in over 100 newspapers and magazines, including Wealth Creator, My Business Magazine, AFR Boss and Virgin's In-flight magazine.

Find out more http://www.businessblueprint.com

If you'd like more sales, customers and leads coming into your business then don't miss out on these FREE books...

"Secrets of Marketing Experts Exposed" and "Secrets of Small Business Owners Exposed"
simply visit http://free.businessblueprint.com/amazing-business-books/

Exercise ~ Sell Me

Start collecting different types of social proof to add to your marketing using the E.N.D.O.R.S.E. Social Proof System.

Expert ~ Which experts can put in a good word for you?
Numbers ~ What facts and figures of your sales or results can you use?
Demonstration ~ How can you demonstrate what you do?
Our Friends ~ How many ways can your friends help promote you?
Relationship ~ How can you start to build a relationship with your clients or how can you strengthen the relationship you have with your existing clients?
Superstar ~ How can you leverage Celebrity power?
End User ~ Do happy clients show people the benefits of working with you?

The Power of Influence and Authority ~ Kat Heart

"Just do video" about ten years ago when I was first looking for a way to make money from home I sunk a cool couple of k in to another home business scam. Although the business side of thing's didn't really pan out how I'd hoped, it was in fact what kick started me to getting to where I am today.

The guy who recruited me taught me 2 key thing's which I took on board and went on to deeper develop.

1. *Marketing psychology* and 2. *The power of influence and authority*.

In my line of work I now teach people how to grow their presence on-line. If you looked at my actual numbers, they're not huge, mostly due to stop starting and a bucket load of other thing's BUT I will tell you whenever I decide to sell something I will make sales within the first 15 minutes and this comes down to the trust and following I have built via Social Media.

Pretty cool right! So what do I do and how do I do it?'

It's a well pieced together combination of trust, influence and authority. When structured properly it can work for you like a well oiled engine, doing the background work for you so that by the time you're ready to sell something people will want to buy from you.

Your story, wins, testimonials, examples, awards, knowledge and skill set displayed properly and used consistently in video, tweets and status updates will over time help you grow a following of people who trust you.

Firstly, prepare to step in to leadership, to stand out and to fight for what you believe in. Sitting on the fence trying to please everybody and not wanting to 'rock the boat' will keep you stuck at the same level as everyone else.

When you make it blatantly obvious, what you do and why you do it people will be able to figure out for themselves that they want to work with you. More often than not I have people tell me that they have known they will work with me for quite some time but have just been waiting for the right opportunity.

Firstly start with the foundations. Who do you serve? How do you serve them? Get clear on that. Secondly, brainstorm out a whole heap of topics you think they would like to hear about, if you get stuck on this use a keyword tool to see what people are searching for online it will give you a ton of content and topic ideas.

Next, start a Facebook business page. Think very carefully what you name this page. What you name your business and / or your social channels does make a difference. The more obvious it is the better you will do.

Now let's put it into action.

1. Video – make videos ASAP. Talk on the topics you have brainstormed. Don't stress about getting it perfect just get it started. Video (when done authentically) will increase the trust factor and position you as a leader.

2. Publish – it doesn't have to be a novel or even your own work. If you can get published as a contributor in someone else's book this is also awesome or get a book of your own on to Amazon / Kindle ASAP. Write on your topic and show this from your Facebook / website. I have now been featured in 3 books. The idea is "wow, she's got a book…. She must know what she's talking about". It puts you in to a position of authority almost instantly.

3. Put your focus on solving solutions. Remember when you're in business you're in the business of solving people's problems.

4. Ensure your sales funnel is in place BEFORE using Social Media to reach people. It's pointless driving traffic if they have nowhere to go and no way to learn from you or buy from you.

Remember, this isn't all going to happen overnight, but if you consistently chip away at it over time you will develop a kick butt online presence and strong foundation to build your empire on.

Kat Heart is the author of Home Business Queen and the founder of Women's Web Marketing and also several Business Women's networks.

In 2009 after the birth of her daughter her world literally falling apart and Kat had to find away to rebuild her life and her income, this is when Women's Web Marketing was born, along with an intense desire to share her story and tech Women why it's so crucial to have alternate income streams in place.

"I am passionate about empowering and supporting Women with the skills, knowledge and mindset to grow their ultimate business.... it's all about living life on **YOUR** own terms!"

Find out more http://katheartinc.com

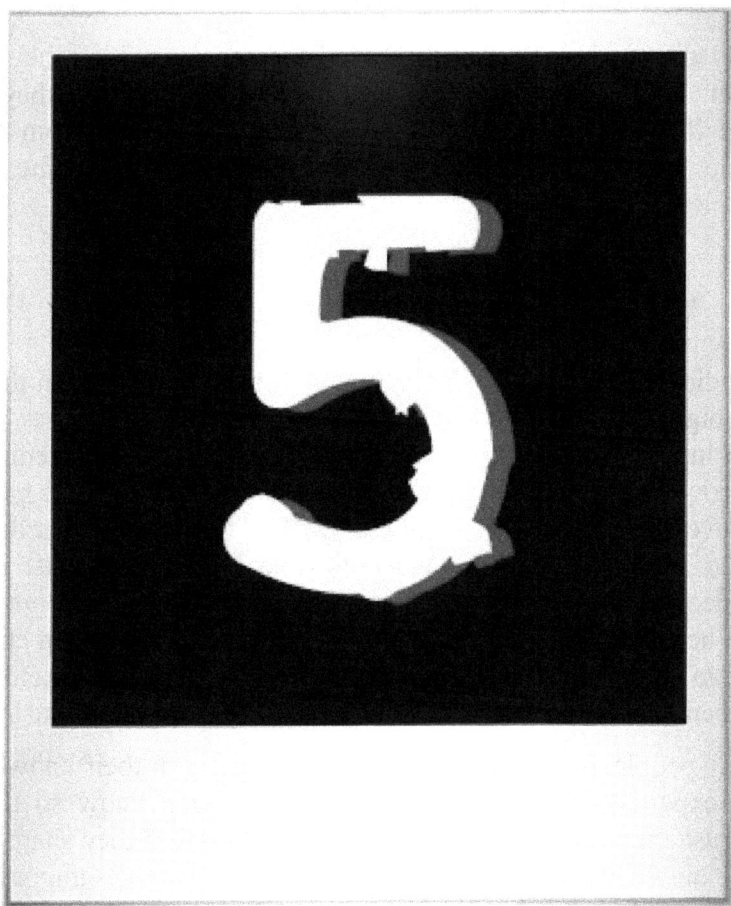

Chapter 5 ~ Teach

The More You Give, The More You Get Back

Many experts believe that they need to keep everything they do a secret. That if they share how they do what they do then they will be inviting the competition in to take their clients away from them. While in rare cases this may be true most of the time it is completely false.

How To Catch Monkeys In India

In India, Monkey hunters use a box with a small opening at the top just big enough for the monkey to slide his hand into. They place nuts in the box so the monkey will reach in to grab them. The monkey reaches in and grabs the nuts making a fist. As he goes to remove his hand from the box the monkey finds the hole at the top is too small to take his hand out while holding the nuts. He is trapped but all he has to do is open his hand, let go of the nuts and then he can fit back through the hole to freedom. He has a choice. Let go of the nuts and be free or hold on to the nuts and stay trapped. Guess what he picks every time? He hangs onto the nuts.

Many people are no different to the monkey with their knowledge and expertise. They hold onto everything they know so tightly because they are scared they will lose something if they share what they know but all they are doing is keeping themselves trapped.

There are two things you need to remember when it comes to teaching others about what you do. One is that only you can deliver your message the way you do it. No one else has what you do and no one else delivers your message like you do. Think about it. Has there been a massage that you have heard several times before from many different people but it was not until you heard it from someone you may have had a connection with that you really heard that message for the first time? Take goal setting for example. Almost every self help coach out there talks about goal setting but each of them has a different way to describe it.

The other thing you need to remember is that people are generally lazy. They would rather pay someone else to do it for them rather than do it themselves.

74

Let's take an example of a lawn mower repair business. I know what you are thinking. *What can they teach without taking away business from themselves?* Let's say they make a series of videos about servicing and taking care of your lawn mower. Even though they service lawn mowers they want to show people how to do it. Now someone at home watched this video on how to service their lawn mower and says, "So that is how you do it. You know what that is a lot of hassle so I will just pay them to service it for me". Now because this business took the time to show them how to do it for themselves they established their expertise in lawn mower repairs and servicing. They now have built trust and credibility in the market place above other lawn mower repair businesses that want to keep people in the dark.

Walk Your Talk

In this era of the abundance of information people are researching a subject and then just teaching what they have learnt. What happens in this situation is that they skip the step of actually implementing what they have learnt to discover for themselves the pitfalls and triumphs of what can happen. Worse than that, some of this information did not work in the first place but because the person who taught it did such a good job of making it sound easy and successful the next person does the exact same thing.

This is where authentic authorities will stand out in the crowd. They are the ones that can not only talk the talk but they walk the walk. You can see their results. They can answer your questions and they have the proof to back up what they say. This is the type of credible expert you want to be.

Types of Teaching

There are many different ways to teach people what you do. A few of them will be covered in more detail in the next chapter. Here is just some of the ways you can teach people to prove your expertise.

Put it in writing

When you put your knowledge down in words that reflect not only your knowledge but your personality in the way you write it, you can teach others while building a massive amount of credibility. This subject is covered in detail in the next chapter but for now here are some of the ways you can teach in writing.

*Write a book
*Publish a blog
*Write articles

Take the Stage

Public Speaking is a fantastic way to not only teach but to build credibility. The minute you step onto that stage you gain credibility. You must be an expert to be standing up there talking down to everyone in the crowd, is the perceived notion when you step up to speak. This credibility can disappear as quickly as it came to you if when you open your mouth you show that you have no idea what you are talking about or your personality comes off as condescending.

I like to call that 'Pompous Presenter Syndrome'. This occurs when the speaker gets up there and acts so much like the expert that you get the feeling that they are truly looking down on you during the talk or after the talk when they are literally on the same level as you. I understand that there needs to be a certain amount of confidence that comes with being the expert but if that comes at the price of being an approachable person then that is someone I do not want to work with.

Teaching In Motion

Videos, webcasts and other forms of media like this are very effective in teaching people. Personally many times I have wanted to learn how to do something so I went to YouTube to find if some smart person has made a video to teach me. It can be a lot easier to learn how to do something if you can see exactly what they are doing rather than trying to work out with words alone.

Another advantage of making videos is that you will be found much easier on Google if you upload them to YouTube. Google owns YouTube and they make a lot of money from the advertising on these videos so if you want to rank on Google quickly you need to be making videos.

From Struggling Single Mum To International Success

Lauren Luke was a 27 year old single mother who wanted a better life for her son. She had an idea to sell cosmetics on eBay. After saving for months she had enough money for her first order of cosmetics from a wholesaler. Wanting to stand out from the competition Laura began to take pictures of the makeup applied rather than just the containers.

Those pictures alone skyrocketed her business with Lauren earning that same amount or even more than her day job as a taxi dispatch clerk. Soon Lauren began receiving hundreds of emails everyday asking how to create the looks shown in her pictures. In 2007 Lauren opened a YouTube account and began making demonstration videos.

Before long, Lauren's videos had reached 1 million views and counting. She was getting requests to make videos showing girls how to create celebrity looks. Due to the success Lauren became the go to expert in this field. In March 2009 the 'By Lauren Luke' makeup line was launched by a New York Cosmetics Company. Lauren now has an app, a book and has made television appearances around the world.

All this from sharing her knowledge and helping everyday women get the celebrity look.

Music to your Brain

You are not limited to video. Some people really don't want to appear in front of the camera. They don't want to make power point slides and have all these extras that are needed to make videos. So, one way that has been around for over 100 years is to teach with your voice. The technology has changed but the message that is delivered is the same.

Through the power of the simple telephone you can run a successful business teaching others. There are people out there today making 6 figures just teaching people through teleseminars. This is where they can get on a conference line and talk with groups of people at the same time, sharing their knowledge. Whether free or paid this method is very effective.

This is not limited to conference calls, there are many successful people teaching on podcasts and iTunes. This makes it easy for people to just download the content to whatever device they use and listen to it at a time that is convenient to them. Traveling to and from work is a really good time to learn something new rather than singing along to the top 40.

Avoid Information Overload

You want to share parts of what you know but not everything. This is not because you are holding this back; it is because you don't want to overwhelm your prospects with information. This will cause them to feel as if what you are teaching is just too complicated and that they will never be able to get the hang of this. You also may weigh them down with so much information that they never get through the free stuff to move on to working with you.

You want to keep it simple. Quick tips and tricks will demonstrate that you know what you are talking about, while giving people useful information that they can implement to help them move forward.

Quizzes and visual aids such as infographics can also be very effective tools.

Information Product Creation

Creating information products such as courses or workshops are a great way to teach and make money at the same time. The beauty of creating information products is you only need to do the work once and you can reap the benefits over and over again.

Information products can include eBooks, eCourses, home study kits, live or virtual workshops, or programs; just to name a few.

Signature System

One of the most powerful tools you can have when you are teaching is a signature system. A signature system is something that is unique to you. It is used to explain or teach what or how you achieve the transformation you offer in an interesting and easy to understand way. For example, the I.N.S.T.A.N.T. Credibility Formula™ is one of my signature systems.

Once you find your own unique signature system you can leverage it to create a signature talk, signature workshop, a book, an online course, a video series and much more.

Here is another one of my signature systems that will help you find yours.

Exercise ~ C.O.I.N. Your Signature System

Step 1: **C**ollect all the information you have to offer. This includes all the tips and tricks, articles, exercises, information and anything you use to do what you do.

Step 2: **O**rganise this information into steps. Group like things together and work out which order everything must go in.

Step 3: **I**dentify the bones of your system. People are often tempted to put everything they know into the system but this is a big mistake. You will overwhelm your customers and clients and this will have the opposite effect than what you are aiming for. What is the minimum amount someone can do to see results?

Step 4: **N**ame your system. This can sometimes be the hardest part but it is very important to get this right. You want something catchy the will intrigue people to want to know more. Some examples of catchy names are acronyms (my favourite) and themes – like dating or shifting gears to go faster.

If you need a little help developing your own unique signature system, I have just the thing for you. The **"Get It D.O.N.E."** package. Simply visit http://www.amandarobins.com/getitdone to find out more.

Chapter 6 ~ Author

#1 Way To Gain Instant Credibility

The number one way to get instant credibility is to write a book. You will be amazed at how many people have dreamed of writing a book so the fact that you actually wrote and published one will give you tremendous trust.

Believe it or not but your book does not have to be long or even really good for that matter for you to get instant credibility from it. I know that sounds weird and for a lot of people I have told this to, a bit of a disappointment but most people will not get past the first chapter. That is not because the book is not readable or good but because they get side tracked. I remember reading that only 5% of all people read a book until the end. This is a fact I keep in mind whenever I finish reading a book. Now take that fact and I bet the percentage of people that start writing a book and never finish it, let alone put it out into the world, is even lower.

Take it from my personal experience writing a book alone is one of the hardest ways to make money. There is leverage in writing a book considering that you only have to write it once and you can sell it over and over again but the problem is you can really only sell the same book once per person and if on the rare occasion they buy more copies, celebrate but usually they lend their copy to their friends. The real money that is made in business is by repeat business. This does not usually happen when it comes to book writing unless you have a book series, which once you write your first book you may rethink. The other problem with relying on book sales is people have a preconceived price of what a book should cost. Somewhere between $10 - $30 is what people believe the book would be worth no matter how beneficial the information in the book may be.

Keeping what I told you in mind I would recommend that every business owner and service provider writes a book. Why? Because writing a book makes you an instant expert in the eyes of your prospect. You need to see your book as a big business card. One that people want to keep, one that makes you more credible just by saying I wrote a book and one that gives people an insight into what you do.

I remember the first time I told someone I was writing a book. They were amazed. That feeling has not gone away. I am also amazed about how many people tell me that they have either written a book or want to write a book but don't know how to go about it. It seems out of reach. Honestly that is what I thought too until I wrote and published my first 2 books. Then watching them become Amazon bestsellers was one of the highlights of 2013 for me.

Just imagine how your credibility will skyrocket when you can hand people a copy of your book at your next networking event as opposed to a plain business card that everyone else is handing out.

Another great advantage of writing a book is that it makes it easier for people searching for someone to help them choose you. Imagine you are looking for a real estate agent to sell your home. You have quite a few to choose from and they all seem to know what they are talking about but there is one that is a little different. That one real estate agent wrote a book called '10 Ways to Sell Your House Fast'. Which one will you choose? The one who wrote the book on the subject, or the ones that are doing the same marketing as everyone else? I would choose the one that wrote the book on the subject because in my eyes they are the expert.

A Practical Novel

While I was researching the best way to write a book, I have picked up some valuable tips for writing a book that people will want to read and remember after they have read it.

When was the last time you sat down a read a textbook for fun? I am not sure about you but I don't think I have ever done that at all. If I did not need to read it I didn't. Personally with books like that I read the bare minimum to get the information I need and then I move on to something else.

When was the last time you read a novel that you couldn't put down? A book that had you wanting more and kept your interest until the very end. This is the type of book you want to write.

Now I know you are not writing a fiction book, you are writing a non-fiction book designed to set you apart from the crowd. While this is true you do not want your book to come out as textbook.

You need to write a practical novel. Your book needs to be an informative practical guide but it needs to be filled with stories that engage your audience. I guarantee that they will forget the steps you have taught them but they will remember the stories you have told.

Think back about this book. Unless you have skipped to this chapter I am assuming you have read the book up until this time. Let me ask you. Can you tell me the first 3 steps that I have taught you? Maybe not. Now let me ask you if you can remember one of the stories that have been told in this book? Chances are your answer will be yes.

One of the first books that I remember reading that had this type of format is "Think and Grow Rich" by Napoleon Hill. While I can't remember the steps in his systems I can remember some of the stories that he shared about how these techniques work. Here is one story that has made a real impact on me.

Three Feet From Gold

One of the most common causes of failure is the habit of quitting when one is overtaken by *temporary defeat.* Every person is guilty of this mistake at one time or another.

An uncle of R. U. Darby was caught by the "gold fever" in the gold-rush days and went west to DIG AND GROW RICH. He had never heard that *more gold has been mined from the brains of men than has ever been taken from the earth.* He staked a claim and went to work with pick and shovel. The going was hard, but his lust for gold was definite.

After weeks of labor, he was rewarded by the discovery of the shining ore. He needed machinery to bring the ore to the surface. Quietly, he covered up the mine, retraced his footsteps to his home in Williamsburg, Maryland, and told his relatives and a few neighbors of the 'strike'. They got together money for the needed machinery, had it shipped. The uncle and Darby went back to work the mine.

The first car of ore was mined, and shipped to a smelter. The returns proved they had one of the richest mines in Colorado! A few more cars of that ore would clear the debts. Then would come the big killing in profits.

Down went the drills! Up went the hopes of Darby and his uncle! Then something happened! The vein of gold ore disappeared! They had come to the end of the rainbow, and the pot of gold was no longer there! They drilled on, desperately trying to pick up the vein again—all to no avail.

Finally, they decided to QUIT.
They sold the machinery to a junk man for a few hundred dollars, and took the train back home. Some "junk" men are dumb, but not this one! He called in a mining engineer to look at the mine and do a little calculating. The engineer advised that the project had failed, because the owners were not familiar with "fault lines" His calculations showed that the vein would be found JUST THREE FEET FROM WHERE THE DARBYS HAD STOPPED DRILLING! That is exactly where it was found!

The 'Junk' man took millions of dollars in ore from the mine, because he knew enough to seek expert counsel before giving up.

Most of the money which went into the machinery was procured through the efforts of R. U. Darby, who was then a very young man. The money came from his relatives and neighbors, because of their faith in him. He paid back every dollar of it, although he was years in doing so.

Long afterward, Mr. Darby recouped his loss many times over, *when he made the discovery* that DESIRE can be transmuted into gold. The discovery came after he went into the business of selling life insurance.

Remembering that he lost a huge fortune, because he STOPPED three feet from gold, Darby profited by the experience in his chosen work, by the simple method of saying to himself, "I stopped three feet from gold, but I will never stop *because men say 'no'* when I ask them to buy insurance."

3 Steps to Write a Practical Novel

The basic format of writing a practical novel is as follows:

1. Make a point or teach something (use your signature system from chapter 5)
2. Reinforce it with a story
3. Write a conclusion tying it all in together

If you are not a good story telling simply ask someone else to write the stories for you or ask them to share their own stories. It does not really matter where they come from as long as they are entertaining.

"One of the most tragic things I know about human nature is that all of us tend to put off living. We are all dreaming of some magical rose garden over the horizon instead of enjoying the roses that are blooming outside our windows today"
~Dale Carnegie

The Power of Publishing ~ Dale Beaumont

One of the most powerful ways to build your profile – online and otherwise - is to write your own book. When you have written a book about your area of knowledge, people literally start to think of you differently. It sounds bizarre I know, but it's true. There is a certain "expert" status that accompanies authors, and by creating that for yourself, you can dramatically increase your profile and credibility.

Let me give you a personal example of this, which will then outline exactly why this is true.

When I had finished high school I began to attend lots of seminars and courses in the area of personal development. I started to learn from the best in the business and while I was there I thought to myself "Wow, this information is amazing, why wasn't I taught this in school?" I even had other attendees at the seminars coming up to me and saying: "You're so lucky. If only I had the chance to learn this information at your age, I wonder where I would be now."

Then came my idea, why not start teaching this information to teenagers? I'm going to take the best of what I have learnt and tailor it in a way that will be fun and stimulating for young people.

So at the age of 19, myself and by good friend Brent Williams ran our very first Tomorrows Youth program in Sydney. But things didn't quite start off the way we had planned. Have a guess at how many people turned up to that first seminar? Only three. Two presenters and only three teenagers. It was pretty disheartening but at the same time we were excited to get the program going so we gave it our all. And slowly it did begin to grow, from three, to six, to 12 and so on.

After three months of expanding, we then we started to hit a brick wall and our attendee numbers just didn't seem to increase past a certain point. This is because by then we had leveraged off all our personal and family networks so the next step was to get out there and start to tap into the mainstream marketplace. Being very naive and knowing very little about business, we thought we could do some advertising. However, once we discovered how expensive it was, we soon realised that this wasn't going to be an option for us, because all of our money was going into running the programs and we had nothing left over for expensive advertising.

Then another person suggested that we try and get some free publicity from our local media. Perfect. So we rung the newspaper and told the reporter our inspiring story. She said: "How old did you say you were?" and I replied that we were 19. She then said: "So at 19-years-of-age, what makes you think you know anything about helping young people?" Then she hung up the phone. Ouch!

Our hearts sank. We were devastated because all of a sudden, someone was putting a limit on what we were doing and telling us that we didn't have the profile and credibility to do the work we so desperately wanted to do. For a few days we really thought about this negative comment and what we were going to do about it. Finally, someone suggested that there is a way that you can manufacture credibility. Sounded pretty good to us so we asked "OK how do you do that?" And their answer was – write a book.

I'm sure you can guess the next step. It took us around four months to write a book called *The World At Your Feet*. It was a personal development book for teenagers, and we were very proud of it (and still are today, of course). Most books that I write these days are around 300 pages long, however, this first book was only tiny at 78 pages. It wasn't substantial at all, but it was just about taking the knowledge that we had learnt and putting it down on paper in a way that teenagers would relate to it.

Then in the space of six months, things finally started to skyrocket. To begin with, our local newspapers and magazines started writing little stories about us and our book. Then, national publications started to pick up the story and the articles got bigger. And after all that, we were asked to appear on *Sunrise*, the major breakfast television show in Australia. Jackpot. We were then interviewed on the *Today* show, Cheeze TV and *Mornings with Kerri-Anne*. The response was huge, and all of a sudden our programs started to fill up.

In that six-month period, we received over $180 000 worth of media exposure. Around 40 to 50 articles were written about us, as well as numerous radio and television interviews. And the best part – it was all free. This enabled Tomorrows Youth to grow from a couple of hundred teenagers to now, as I write this, over 23,500 young people through our seminars in five different countries.

Now are you starting to see why writing your own book can be so important when trying to build your profile? That book gave us the permission and authority to reach and impact far more people than we were doing on our own. Nothing had changed, we were still 19-years-old, but suddenly people began to take notice because "if they can write a book about it, they must really know what they are talking about".

Our book also gave us a massive amount of credibility and we have leveraged that credibility to attract bigger and better opportunities throughout the growth and development of Tomorrows Youth.

I used this strategy again in my mid-20s when I embarked on creating my *Secrets Exposed* series. I wrote four books to begin with, all at the same time so that I could release them almost one after the other and build momentum. Then once they were finished, they were released to the marketplace. Now check out this photo taken in Sydney Airport bookstore and have a look at the other books that are surrounding mine…

Talk about in good company. One of the books right next to mine is by Robert Kyosaki, the world's number one finance expert. Another is by Richard Branson, need I say more? And Seth Godin, a global leader in business marketing. And there I am, smack bang in the middle of this amazing talent with my four books. That's what I call credibility. Twenty-five years of age and surrounded by the best in the business.

Following the release of those four books, I stepped it up a notch and released 11 new titles in one year. Want to know the secret to how I finished so many in a single year? Hard work. That's it, I worked really, really hard, with long hours and no holidays. It was a crazy year but I had my *why* in sight. I knew that when I had finished I wanted to spend more time with my growing family travelling around the world, and these books were going to give me that opportunity so there was no giving up.

At the end of that year, I had written 16 books and I was only 26 years old. I don't say this to show off at all, I only say it because I hope it makes you realise that the possibilities for your business are endless, and if I can do it, you can too.

Since releasing the *Secrets Exposed* series, we have sold over 250 000 copies into the market, and they have launched my career. Each book has my blood, sweat and tears inside it, but the end result makes it all very worth it. The books generated a fantastic income, and have allowed me to travel the world with my family. The month after the last *Secrets Exposed* book was released, my son Finnegan was born. At the time of writing this he is 22 months old and we have already taken him to over 25 different countries.

You may be thinking at this point "that's ok for you but what can I write a book about?" Well there are thousands of potential topics and an infinite number of stories you could share, but I always say – start with what you know.

Do you realise that you are paid because of something that you know? You have information in your head right now that most others don't and if you can take that information and document it in a book, then other people will pay you money to access that information.

Before I move on to the second strategy that can propel your profile, I want to give you another quick example of why writing a book is such an important step. I understand that sometimes my story can be slightly overwhelming, so let me tell you about a friend of mine called Tony Melvin.

Tony is an accountant and one day during a meeting he said to me: "Does this writing a book stuff actually work?" Of course my answer was yes. So Tony decided to do something to propel his profile and raise the awareness of his business. He wrote a book called *How to Legally Reduce Your Tax*. It's a whole book about tax. No offence of course to any accountants that might be reading this, but I am simply saying it's not exactly a topic that ignites a fire in most people.

Well of course I was proved wrong, and Tony sold over one hundred thousand copies. All he was doing was putting the knowledge he already had down on paper, but people were digesting it and loving it. He went on to write a second book and then a third. From these books being released into the marketplace, he was getting around 30-40 new business calls per week. These books took Tony's business from $2.5 million to over $10 million a year in turnover in under two years. Talk about double your income.

Tony self-published those first books and now a major publishing company called HarperCollins has approached him and has just bought the rights to his book series. Tony is an amazing story, but this can be your story too. If you have a passion for something, and the knowledge to back it up, why not put it on paper.

Remember you don't necessarily need to be the *number one* expert about your subject, but once you have written the book, what's important is that you will then appear to be.

So now you know why it is so important to write a book, let me go through the how. Clearly I could write an entire book about this one subject, because there is a lot of information to understand, but I will just run through some of the basics.

- **Find yourself a great editor** – I am by no means a fantastic writer, in fact, I'm dyslexic. But if you have a great editor they can take your basic ideas and make them sound amazing.

- **Ask around for help** – When thinking, for example, about the title of your book, ask your family and friends for help or even your database. You should brainstorm a list yourself then ask others for their opinion.

- **Invest in professionals** – Once your book has been edited it needs to be designed and printed. In the front of other books you will see contact details for this and also you can search for more online. These people know what they are doing and they have the skills to make your book look fantastic in print.

- **Do your research first** – If you are choosing to self-publish your book, research distributors. They can then sell your book into the bookstores for you, as nine times out of ten bookstores will not take books straight from the author themselves.

- **Finally, don't think book, think book series** – When you initially come up with your idea for a book, try and turn that into three or four books. This way, you can continue to grow your readership, package your books together and leverage off the readers who bought your first book.

Dale Beaumont

Dale Beaumont is one of Australia's most successful young entrepreneurs. Having built three different million-dollar businesses before the age of thirty, today Dale is the founder and CEO of Business Blueprint®, the world's most forward-thinking business education company.

Dale is also the author and publisher of 16 best-selling books, which have collectively sold over a quarter of a million copies. Incredibly, 11 of those 16 books were published in a single year, a feat that earned him the title "Australia Most Prolific Author".

As a result of Dale's success, he has been interviewed on Sunrise, Today Show, Mornings with Kerri-Anne, Ten News, ABC Radio, Radio 2UE as well as being featured in over 100 newspapers and magazines, including Wealth Creator, My Business Magazine, AFR Boss and Virgin's In-flight magazine.

Find out more http://www.businessblueprint.com

You Don't Have To Do It Alone

Writing your first book can seem like an impossible task. Either you don't feel like you have anything important to say or you may feel that no one will be interested in reading anything from you so you just don't write.

There is good news. You are not alone. You don't have to make it all about you. You can get other people to contribute to your book or even better write the whole thing for you. Sounds too good to be true? It isn't. This is how many people get their names and knowledge published. You will be amazed at the people that are willing to write something for your book or even better you can simply interview them over the phone, record it, get it transcribed and bam you have a book. Even better than that they may even market your book with you. Can you imagine having 10 people promoting your book at the same time? How many more people could you reach with your message?

You can also make a compilation book. Jack Canfield and Mark Victor Hansen did just this with their "Chicken Soup" series. They got people from all around the world to submit their stories and picked the best ones to appear in the book, printed them and sold them. Boy did they sell them. The book series has sold over 500 million copies in over 100 countries.

You can do the same thing. There are thousands of people out there who want to appear in a book. You can hold a competition for people to send in their stories and tips. You then pick the best ones and make them into a book. Very simple, yet very effective.

Even easier than that is to appear in someone else's book. You could write a chapter, tell a story or you could use your experience to be a case study within their book.

Don't Stop At A book

For some people a book is either too hard so they never write one or they stop at just a book.

While writing a book can be one of the best ways to gain instant credibility, you are not limited to only writing a book. Here are a couple of ways to get instant credibility in print.

Write articles

Writing articles for magazines, newspapers, newsletters and even online publications can boost your credibility.

Publish a blog

In the modern day having a blog can be a must for any online business. Not only can you show your expertise and create a loyal following, you also get your website to rank higher on Google.

"Credibility's About Connection" ~ Justin Herald

I was approached to write a book, it was sort of at the end of *Attitude* I guess where the media were going through the roof with me starting the business and then selling it. I said, "Okay, I'll give it a shot" plus everyone wanted me to. So, I had three publishers approach me in the same week which apparently is fairly rare.

They all wanted me to write an autobiography. I said to them that I hadn't had a life yet so I can't write about it, then I suggested I write the first book which was "Would You Like Attitude With That?" the way that I wanted to write it. Originally, the publishers said that it wouldn't work but they had to do it anyway and that book went bestseller after three weeks, which was pretty cool. After my first book they gave me an eight book deal on my fourth week.

I didn't know I could write a book and a week and a half later, I take the book back in a big envelope and go, "Here it is." They said, "What's that, your first chapter?" I said, "No, that's the whole book." They said, "Well, it normally takes people a long time to write a book." I replied, "You should have told me that before I wrote the book, I would've taken a long time."

I didn't know I had that skill and I think the biggest issue with anything when it comes to growing a business or success, is people struggle because they think too much. When it comes to writing a book, I think you just let it flow and just talk from the inside of you and then go back and look at it but not try to perfect it right from the start. Don't try to put fancy shmancy words in there that other people may know but you would have no idea what it means if you were asked especially by the media. That's the one thing that I do well because the media will always pick a certain part of a book and talk about it and if I don't know what I've written, nor if it hasn't come from how I would say it, then it's not going to be congruent. So I think if people are going to write a book, just do it from your own personality and that's what people are attracted to anyway.

Obviously if you write a book and you get good publicity from it from a media perspective, it sort of takes a life of its own and by default, the credibility comes. That is one thing that happens when you write a book, is you do become credible. That's just sort of the gift with purchase, which I found out later on.

But I think with any book if you want credibility, it's got to actually say something that people may have heard before but you have to just say it in a different way.

I've got some people that come to me and want me to mentor them. All they want to do is write a book and when I ask them why, it's so they get known and I have to sort of gently, or sometimes not, let them know that if that's your big plan, it's not going to work.

It's a business. It's a tool, not just writing a book, I know exactly how my books sell. I know where they should be positioned in the bookstore and it's not within the 'wealth creation' section. They always put my books under 'wealth creation'. I never wrote about how to make money. Well one of them I did write about on how to grow a business without spending any money but that was on how not to spend money.

There are a lot of people now and I mean I talk to a lot of them during my coaching courses that, want to write a book so people know who they are. I sort of never went into it that way. I think writing a book just to become credible is probably a very short-lived experience.

I was driving down the freeway and this guy cut me off. I sped up and as I drove besides him, I gave him a mouthful. He reached down as he's driving along, held up my book and says, "I love your new book."

There are a lot of people that just want to write a book and they think they've got something to say. I sort of don't agree with that. I think there's got to be something of substance behind you before you write the book.

The reality is no one's reinventing the wheel these days and for me, it's all about making it simpler and making the wheel roll better. Just making by it simpler, I want people to get it. I'm not sure if you've ever read a book and you have to read the same sentence five times to actually figure out what the hell they mean.

Well, this is where when writing a book you've got to actually put yourself into the shoes of the people reading instead of trying to get them to come into your shoes. Same with speaking. I'm not sure how many people you've heard speak, but you hear some people speak and you go, " You're actually preaching at me, you're talking at me not to me." where I want people to sit there and go, "Actually, I could do this, this guy is just like me, he's an idiot just like me" and that way you have more connection.

See, credibility's about connection. It doesn't matter what you've done as far as writing books, getting on stage, being in the media, you can do all of that but if there's no connection with the audience, it's irrelevant. So, that's where credibility and likeability is probably the same thing. There are people that have got a lot of credibility on certain subjects but they're just not likeable people and so I actually think that actually undoes their credibility.

Remember, if you're not congruent with your message, people will work it out and it's going to blow up in your face big time.

Justin Herald has fast become one of the rising stars in the fields of business and personal development. At the age of 25 with only $50 to his name, Justin Herald set about changing the course of his life. Justin created Attitude Inc, a clothing brand that became an international licensing success that turned over millions per year.

Justin's success was so well noted that he was named the "INTERNATIONAL ENTREPRENEUR OF THE YEAR" for 2005. He recently was also awarded the Future Leaders Award, which recognises him as being one of the 50 most influential leaders of the next generation in Australia.

In addition to the success of Attitude Gear®, Justin has produced his own products. Justin first released his business/motivational book in April 2003. Within 3 weeks "Would you like Attitude with that?" hit the bestsellers list. Justin's much anticipated sequel, "So what are you waiting for?", was released in May 2004 with an overwhelming response. He has gone on to write another 6 more best-selling books.

Find out more http://www.justinherald.com

"The reason a lot of people do not recognize opportunity is because it usually goes around wearing overalls looking like hard work."

~Thomas A. Edison

InstantCredibility.com.au

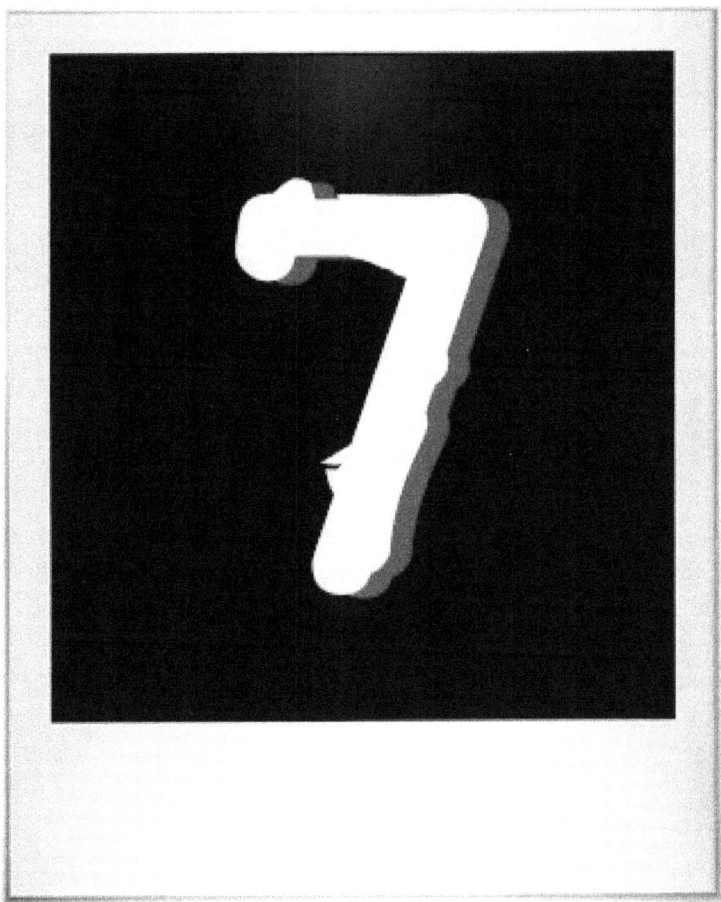

Chapter 7 ~ Newsworthy

Getting People Talking About You

In everyday life the last thing you want is to have people talking about you but in business it is the exact opposite. You want to have people talking about you, in a positive way of course, but you want them talking. If they are talking about you and your business then the competition falls by the way side.

One of the most powerful ways to get credible attention for your business is by appearing in the media. It can be a whole story about what you are doing or you could be a guest expert on a subject that the media is covering at the time.

It does not matter if it is television, radio or in print. The more places you can get your message out the better.

It may seem like an impossible task to get the media to pay attention to you but one thing you need to know is the editors and producers need you just as much as you need them. They have pages to fill, hours of airtime to fill and they need to make it all interesting to keep their audiences intrigued. So if you come along with a relevant story or you have expertise to contribute to a story they are covering then they want to hear from you.

I have a friend who appeared as an expert in a story on *'A Current Affair'*. They simply Googled a topic that her business specialized in and her website was the first one to appear. They called her and asked if she could appear in a segment on the show, which she did. From one short segment on ACA her business made over $20,000 that night. Not bad for a 5 minute story.

"When dealing with people, remember you are not dealing with creatures of logic, but creatures of emotion"
~Dale Carnegie

"The Media Has Changed My Life" ~ Sue Papadoulis

The media world of TV, radio, newspapers, magazines and digital news has given me many things. Most importantly it led me on a career path that sparked an amazing journey culminating in the business I run today, Publicity for Profit.

I've experienced every side of the media industry – as a journalist, then as a public relations manager and finally as a small business owner who managed to score national TV coverage that skyrocketed my business.

As a journalist and News Editor for 10 years I reported on the world's events, some inspiring but many shocking and disturbing. In a major 'aha' moment, I realised journalism was no longer for me, and made the decision to move into one of the only other career options available – public relations.

While I was generating millions of dollars of free publicity for my clients, it still wasn't enough. I wanted more from life. I wanted to inspire others to step up, reach higher and play a bigger game.

I launched a membership web site, which reaped the rewards of exposure on the national program, *A Current Affair*. That three minute segment on TV brought me an instant database of clients and an injection of $40,000 in revenue. So, I know first-hand what it's like to be on the receiving end of publicity. It means massive credibility and instant sales.

It is a great blessing to me to have found my place in the world, where my knowledge about the media and how a journalist's mind works can now be used to help entrepreneurs grow their businesses. I have managed to turn my experience of the media from one that was largely negative, into a force for good – not just for me, but for so many others.

I can't tell you how excited I get when I see the results of our students, and how being in the media is turning their businesses around, as well as providing them great credibility and self belief.

Sue Papadoulis

As a journalist by trade with a 22 year career in the media, Sue understands the media industry inside and out.
She has worked as:
- A News Editor
- A Public Relations Executive
- A PR consultant with her own PR business
- And - Sue has used the media to promote her own businesses, appearing on A Current Affair

Sue now empowers entrepreneurs with all the skills necessary to get their own free publicity in the media.

Her students have appeared on most major TV programs such as Sunrise, The Project, Today Tonight, A Current Affair, Wake Up, Channel 7's Morning Show and Sky Business News.

Sue's goal in life is to inspire others to step up and play a bigger game by using the power of the media.
She is the celebrated co-author of two books – including the Amazon best-seller *"Align, Expand and Succeed"* and *"Ignite Your Business Mojo."*

Web site: www.publicityforprofit.com.au

Newsworthy Strategies

Here are some simple ways to get into the media.

1. Write a Press Release

Chances are the press will not chase you so you have to put your story in front of them. Press Releases are a great way to do just this.

Here are the top 7 tips for increasing the success of your press releases.

1. **Make the story relevant**. If you have an opinion or can help someone with a topic of concern right now the chances of your press release being noticed increase. For example, if you have tips for saving money on your tax return you can send out a press release in June and July when tax season is upon us. You also need to answer the 5 W's. Who, What, Where, Why and When. You can go an extra step further and add the 'How' or back up your story with proof like statistics, etc.

2. **Make contacting you easy.** When you write your press release have your contact information easily accessible. It is a busy time trying to get the stories out on a deadline and they do not have time to chase you down. Put your contact details at the top of your press release.

3. **Catch their eye.** You have to do more than just send out an email that says, "Press Release". You need to make it catchy and worth their attention. They would get hundreds of press releases every week and you need to make yours stand out. Make the most of your headline. Think like a reporter. What headlines stand out to you when you walk past a magazine stand? This is the type of headline you want in your press release.

4. **Pick the right audience.** Do your research when it comes to finding the right media to send your press releases to. You would be wasting your time if you wrote an article on business and sent it to a baby magazine. You want to keep the body of your press release brief and relevant to what their audience wants.

5. **It is not all about you.** I know this sounds a little weird as you are writing a press release to promote your business but what you have to realize is that it is not about you. It is about the reader and how you can help them. What problems are they facing and what solutions can you offer

to help them. If you come at it from this point of view you will have a higher success rate not only with press releases but your overall marketing campaigns.

6. **Build a relationship.** If you come in looking for a one night stand you will be disappointed. You need to build a relationship with reporters and producers. As with other methods throughout this book building a relationship based on trust and respect is vital to increasing your exposure. Just imagine. It is 4pm and their deadline is at 5pm and they are short an expert opinion. Who are they going to call? The person who has helped them and kept in touch with them to be of service, or the person who sent in a press release talking about themselves?

7. **Be Consistent.** If at first you don't succeed try, try, and try again. You may not get your first story in or maybe not even your tenth but you have to keep trying. Whatever the reason as to why you have not attracted the attention you wanted does not mean it will not come. Try calling the reporter or producer and ask them what you can do to make your press releases better, or you could ask them what kinds of stories they are looking for. Remember the squeakiest wheel get the most attention.

2. Offer your Expertise

Call reporters and producers to offer your services. Tell them about your book, blog or anything else that shows you know what you are talking about and then offer your services if they are looking for a guest. The last step is to make yourself available. You may not get a lot of notice before you are asked to be a guest so make sure you are ready with something relevant to say when the call arises.

3. Hold an Event

Make your own news. Create an event that gets attention. You can do many things that tie into your business that people will be interested in.

Here are a few:

* Have a book release party
* Break a world record
* Raise money for charity
* Host a free workshop

Exercise ~ Interview Me

Write a list of reasons why the media will take notice of you.

Make a list of events you could use to leverage for media attention.

Research possible media outlets to promote your business to.

Amazingly Awarding

A powerful way to set you apart as a credible expert is with Awards.

The best part of this technique is you don't have to win to gain credibility. While being able to say you are the winner of the award, which you are aiming for, you can use 'Nominated For' and still receive a boost to your credibility. Think about how many actors are only nominated for an academy award but they still use this in their marketing, after all just being nominated is a great honour.

There are several ways awards can impact your business.

Awards can provide validation and credibility for your business. When a third party has looked at your business, compared it to your competitors, and decided that you deserve to win this makes a powerful statement that you are the best in your industry.

The awards themselves come with their own brand. They have a reputation behind them that make that award important. Once you either win or are nominated for an award you then benefit from that award's brand and credibility.

As you should be looking for ways to be newsworthy, being nominated for an award is something that you can promote then if you win you get to promote yourself all over again. People like to hear about awards. Take the Oscars for example. It is a big news event from the release of the nominations to the red carpet to finally the winners. It is a talked about experience for months and then all the winners and nominees use that information for years to come.

Exercise ~ Award Me

Make a list of awards you can nominate yourself for.

Make a list of awards you have been nominated for or won.

From humble beginnings... ~ Simone Eyles

What started as an idea between two mates "wouldn't it be cool to order a coffee from your phone" is now a global smart ordering platform.

365cups allows businesses to extend their service beyond their bricks and mortar front door. What started as a coffee ordering App is now a platform for boutique cafes and retail giants to put their products in their customers pockets, so they can "order, pickup and go"

With a HQ in Wagga Wagga regional NSW, 365cups is proud to be providing such a tech solution to clients all around the globe. With a global client and user base, 365cups is agile and always evolving yet still looking after their clients and customers with some good old fashioned country service.

From humble beginnings 365cups is proud to have achieved some significant milestone as well as win some prestigious awards. The first award 365cups won was the "Best App Food and Drink" at the Australian Mobile Awards, an honour, seeing the competitors.

365cups had a global vision from the start, and has worked very hard to build up their client base and brand awareness, by being active and contributing to the tech community and immersing themselves in the industry 365cups are now often sought out as thought leaders on the topic all things mobile ordering. This opportunity allows for 365cups to receive great editorial and media representation, invaluable exposure that money can't buy.

An example of this is when 365cups was featured on 60 Minutes, in a store about the "App Revolution" this story gave 365cups incredible exposure and instant credibility when featured alongside some of the globes greatest App Developers.

365cups is now working on some new and exciting projects with global brands and government, it is exciting times as we experience rapid growth and we never know who will contact us and want us to do some work for them.

365cups will attend the NSW Telstra Business Awards in a few weeks, as they are finalists in best Micro Business and Best Regional Business and Simone has also been nominated for a Telstra Women's Business Award, what an honour!

Simone Eyles, co-founder and director 365cups

Simone Eyles is the Co-founder of leading smart ordering company 365cups.com. The mobile ordering platform changing the way you order, breakfast, lunch, coffee and tea!

Since 2011, my business focus has been 365cups.com, which combines my love of hot caffeinated beverages, technology and people. 365cups is a mobile food and beverage ordering platform, with a focus on coffee (of course!), that connects cafes and customers. Since going live, we have achieved the following outcomes:

• **WINNER Best App Food & Drink 2012 - 2013** Australian Mobile Awards
• **WINNER Excellence in Innovation** Murray-Riverina Business Awards - NSW Business Chamber
• More than 45,000 app users
• Over 150 clients across Australia and New Zealand
• Over 500,000 orders through the system
• Over $4M in revenue generated for our clients

Find out more http://365cups.com

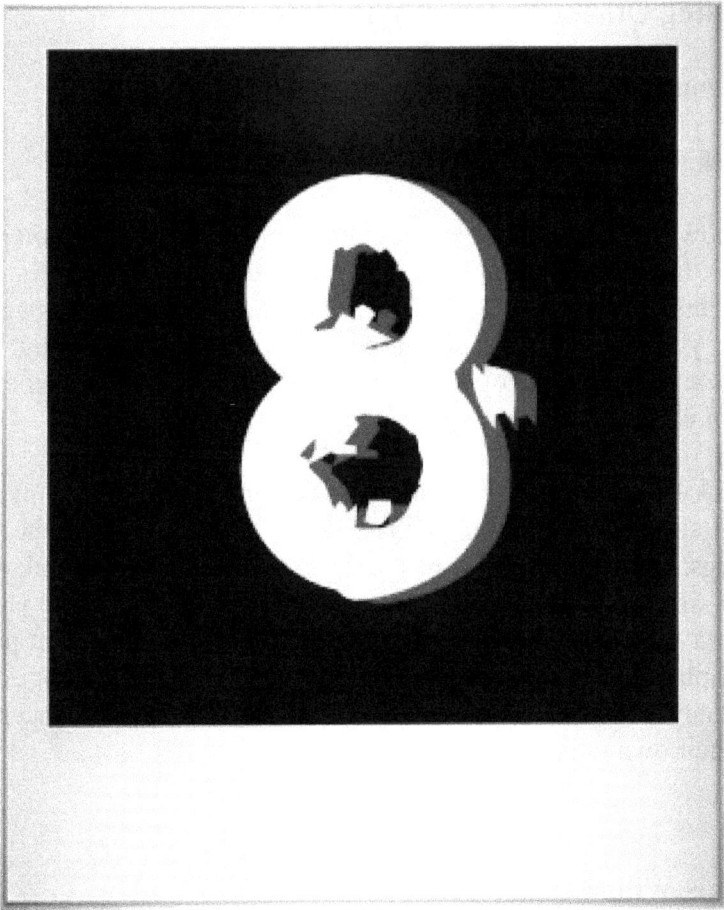

Chapter 8 ~
Team Up

Getting Others To Work With You

Do you know the best way to eliminate your competition?

Work with them.

I know it sounds a little strange but I believe firstly that you really don't have competition. You have people that do similar things to you but they are not you. Only you can deliver your message the way you do, only you can teach the systems the way you know how and there are people out there that can only hear that message from you.

Think back for a minute to a time when an expert taught you about goal setting. Now think of the next person who taught the same things. Keep going to the next and then the next. Now think of the first time your truly heard that message. Think of the time when it was a true 'aha' moment. It could have been the way that person had phrased it or just simple timing that made the message stick. Whatever the reason, everyone taught the same basic concept but in their own unique way.

"This Will Make It Better"

At the Seattle Special Olympics a few years ago, nine physically or mentally disabled athletes assembled at the starting of the 100-yard dash.

The starting pistol sounded and the race began. It was not exactly a dash but each athlete tried their hardest to finish and win the race. Everyone was off except for one little boy, who tripped over on the asphalt, tumbled a few times and then lay on the ground crying. The other eight people in the race heard the boy and slowed down to look back. Seeing the boy in distress each one of them stopped racing and went back to see if he was alright.

One of the athletes, a girl with Down's syndrome, bent down and kissed the boy. "This will make it better", she told him. She helped

110

him up and then all nine contestants linked arms and walked together across the finish line. Everyone in the stadium stood up and cheered for several minutes for this display of kindness.

Together people can achieve great and wonderful things even if they are in a competition.

Working together not only do you take away the feeling of competition when you join together with other businesses, you create a tremendous amount of leverage and power, like the example of co-authoring a book. Imagine if you have 2 businesses promoting each other rather than just you alone promoting yourself, now multiply that by 10. Can you see the power?

Not only do you tap into the power of promotion you can also access the power of the mastermind.

Napoleon Hill defines the "Master Mind" as "Coordination of knowledge and effort, in a spirit of harmony, between two or more people, for the attainment of a definite purpose." He goes on to explain how when two or more minds can come together, something similar to a 'third mind' is created where you can tap into the ideas floating around in the energy of the universe.

It sounds a little weird at first but once you get a chance to use the power of the mastermind for yourself you will be amazed.

Coming together with other like-minded business owners can create ideas and plans that you never thought possible. It can also help you to find solutions to problems that you may be facing.

I have been a part of several mastermind groups throughout the last 10 years and they have been some of the most rewarding experiences of my life. I find it easy to look at other people's business problems and tell them what solutions they can use but it is not so easy to see your own. Think of it like the tip of your nose. You know it is there, everyone else can see it, you can put your finger on it but you can't see it yourself. It can be the same way with your business so using the power of the mastermind to get fresh eyes on your business can really benefit you.

Types of Joint Ventures

Teaming up with other experts can be a very rewarding way to increase your credibility and be noticed by other people interested in what you do.

When was the last time you wanted learn something new? Let's take wealth creation for example. A topic which I love. Did you buy just one book on the subject or did you listen to just one expert? I bet you read, watched and listened to everything you could get your hands on. Why? Because each and every person tells you something different.

So when you are looking at making a name for yourself, think about this. If your potential clients are looking to learn or use what you do and know, they will search for as much information and expertise as they can find. Why not then put it all in the one place?

This is the power of Joint Ventures. Not only can you bring in the collective knowledge and expertise together you also bring the network of people to either buy or promote you.

Let's go over some of the ways you can use joint ventures.

Co-author

Appearing in a book together with leading experts can skyrocket your credibility and as discussed in chapter 6 lightens the workload of writing a book by yourself.

Co-host

Radio, television, print media and in-person events are just some of the ways you can team up with someone else to demonstrate your expertise and boost your credibility. Take talk shows for example. You really need two people to interact with each other in order to make the show interesting. Each person comes with their own point of view which can clash sometimes but it enables the audience to feel a part of the show by either agreeing or disagreeing with what is being said.

Another way this works is by different types of businesses coming together to create a workshop, for example, that covers a range of topics faced by a group of people, e.g. An accountant, business coach and lawyer coming together to hold a workshop for people wanting to start a business.

Telesummit

Telesummits are very popular in the internet marketing world. What they do is bring together many different experts in a certain area, each with their own area of expertise and they give a short presentation as part of the whole event. It can be held all on the one day or over separate days and even weeks. Each expert involved not only shares their knowledge but also promotes the whole event.

Exercise ~ Join Me

Make a list of people you can team up with.

Start connecting with people you could joint venture with. Build the relationship starting now.

Power of Promotion

As with 'social proof' having someone else promote you can be a powerful way to gain instant trust in the eyes of potential clients. If you get an email from someone you trust letting you know that a friend of theirs is launching a new product, you are more inclined to have a look than if you saw a random ad somewhere.

In this electronic age this power has never been easier to use. Through websites, emails and other forms of media you can tap into the power of affiliates.

Affiliates are people that promote your business and when someone buys your product or service you pay them a commission. Commissions are usually a capped price or a percentage of what the new client has paid to you. The beauty of this is if no one buys you don't pay a cent and if you do get new business you get paid first and then you pay your affiliates.

Unlike most forms of advertising which requires you to pay up front to promote your business if you make any money from that advertisement or not, with affiliate marketing if you are not making money it does not cost you anything.

Treat this form of promotion like any other marketing you do in your business. You need to teach your affiliates exactly how to market your products and services. Provide them with templates, guidelines and training that will attract the clients you want. While they may mean well if an affiliate goes out gung-ho and is really pushy trying to sell your products and service it can really affect your reputation and credibility in a negative way.

Exercise ~ Promote Me

Make a list of projects you either have or can launch that you could use affiliate marketing to promote.

Create an affiliate program.

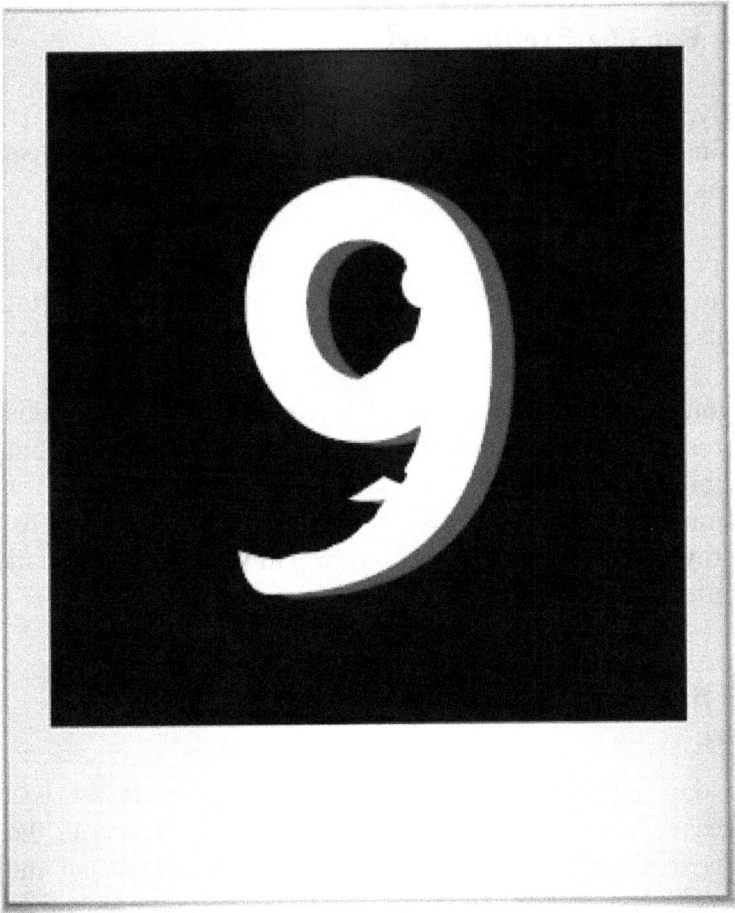

Chapter 9 ~ Putting It All Together

Now For The Exciting Part

Firstly, congratulations for getting this far in the book. I know personally it is a pretty big achievement to get to the last chapter of a book.

I hope you have learnt some new and interesting ways to get instant credibility. Now is the time when you pull it all together and use what you have learnt.

As you read through the book there were many exercises designed to create awareness and give you a kick start to climbing the credibility staircase. If you have not done them yet I highly recommend you go back and do them now as I am about to show you my way of using these techniques in your business, marketing and life.

The Burning Desire

One day a young man asked Socrates, "What is the secret to success?" Socrates told the young man to meet him near the river the next morning. The boy did as Socrates asked and the next morning they met at the river. They walked down into the water and when the water got up to their necks, Socrates took the young man by surprise, grabbed the back of his head and pushed it under the water. The boy struggled to get his head above the water but Socrates held on tightly keeping the boy's head down until he started to turn blue. Socrates pulled the boy's head out of the water. The boy gasped for air, took a deep breath and looked at Socrates puzzled. "What did you want the most when you were under the water?" Socrates asked. "Air" the boy replied. "That is the secret to success. When you want success as badly as you wanted air, then you will get it. There is no other secret," exclaimed Socrates.

A burning desire is the starting point of all accomplishment.

Just like a small fire cannot give much heat, a weak desire cannot produce great results...

Did you Google yourself?

If not do it now or if you did what did you find?

Putting The I.N.S.T.A.N.T. Credibility Formula In Action

Step 1 ~ Identity

Inspire Me ~ Once you have a collection of stories share these in your emails, blog posts, books, speaking engagements, social media posts and any other time you interact with people. A great storyteller keeps people intrigued and coming back for more. This is what your stories will do and at the same time they share your expertise in a very appealing way.

Remember Me ~ What do you want to be known for? What is your niche in the market place?

Once you have completed this exercise you need to put this everywhere. If you have decided to be the "Queen of Productivity" for example then you need to refer to yourself as that every time you speak. It needs to be on all your marketing including your websites, business cards, social media, content and anything else you put out into the market place until people start to refer to you as that.

Work With Me ~ Make a list of the qualities that your ideal clients have and make sure you tell people. If they can identify with those qualities and truly feel that they are suited to work with you they will come running. It is not good to just keep the list to yourself, tell the world and then hand choose the best of the bunch.

Transform Me ~ Your marketing will now center around the transformation you provide. You will no longer sell coaching for example but you will sell focus, clarity and accountability.

Fascinate Me ~ What personality are you adding to your business? If you are bold and fun to work with that needs to be reflected in everything you do or if you are professional and respected this should be reflected in everything you do. Remember people are watching what you do so use that to turn on the ideal client magnet.

Impress Me ~ This is where you want to show off your expertise. Come from a point of service. Give and they will return the favour but if you go at it in a selfish way you will repel everyone you come across. Ways to do this can include joining forums and groups so you can answer questions that have been asked. You can add useful information to help people and as you do this they will begin to look at you as the expert and want more. A word of warning: it is very easy to fall into the trap of giving away your knowledge and expertise in return for the kudos. For example you may give a great speech and have someone to pat you on the back and say, "That was a fantastic Speech." Then you hope that by showing how smart you are that will then turn into business. The fact is it will not. Personally I used to fall into this trap. You must first value what you do and even though sometimes you can help for free you deserve to be paid because you really do provide value. You need to find the line between impressing people and selling yourself short.

"Never be afraid to ask for what you are worth."
~ Amanda Robins

Confident Me ~ If you are not ready to step into the spotlight and feel as if you are the expert it will show. Once you have the confidence you need to be known as the expert you will be amazed at what you can do. Work on this day by day. Notice what people are saying about and to you. View yourself through your clients eyes instead of your own, as we are the hardest on ourselves. Day by day you will feel more confident until one day being the expert is normal.

Step 2 ~ Names

Employed Me ~ Now you have your list of employers you can add these to your marketing in a number of ways. Listing them on

LinkedIn, social media and your website is one way. Something a little more subtle is to tell stories about when you worked with these employers. For example you could write a blog post, '5 Lessons I Learnt Working At Fred's Computers'. Do not give away trade secrets or personal information but do tell about your personal growth or how you admire the way they look after their staff, etc.

Mentor Me ~ You can use this list of names similar to the ones above. Share the things you have learnt from these mentors in stories and when you are teaching, paying close attention not to rip off their systems.

Relate To Me ~ Once you have a collection of stories share them in your emails, blog posts, books, speaking engagements, social media posts and any other time you want to prove the point you're teaching. Don't just stop at the stories you have collected. Keep an eye on the media so that you can use the latest stories to create new and relevant stories that keep your prospects and clients engaged with what you are doing.

Compare Me ~ As with your identity use this comparison every chance you get so people can easily begin to draw the comparison between you and who you are comparing yourself to.

See Me ~ Pictures can be very powerful especially when it comes to places like Facebook. So as you get the opportunity to meet and take pictures with celebrities, industry leaders and even your clients, share these. Nothing says I am walking the talk like a picture.

Step 3 ~ Social Proof

Sell Me ~ Your social proof is very powerful and most of the time cannot be used enough.

Step 4 ~ Teach

Teach Me ~ Share your knowledge. Create a web TV show, write a book, blog, networking or just answer questions on forums and Facebook groups.

C.O.I.N. Your Signature System ~ Once you have C.O.I.N.ed your signature system use it in your marketing by leveraging it into a talk, book, workshop, course or any other way you can think of.

Step 5 ~ Author

Read Me ~ Writing is like any other skill you have had to learn. It takes time and practice. The best way to get started is to set aside time each day and just write. Most of what you write you will think is complete crap but that is ok. You will find your voice at some point and you will never look back. Get into print any way you can and if you really can't write remember that you can always pay someone to do it for you.

Step 6 ~ Newsworthy

Talk About Me ~ Stay alert for stories that are relevant to what you do. Create reasons why the media should pay attention to you and let them know. When you do get the media attention you want use it by adding "As Seen On", "Featured In" or "Appeared For" and then list the names of the media you appeared in. Use this on your websites and other marketing to leverage your coverage to boost your credibility.

Interview Me ~ Contact reporters and producers to offer your services as an expert. Make sure you are available to be interviewed and share your expertise.

Award Me ~ Nominate yourself for awards or get someone else to do it for you, if the award requires that. Then if you make it as a finalist, promote that and if you win promote that too. Whether you are a finalist or the winner, you know what to add to your marketing. Put it in your bios, in the signature of your emails, on your website and anywhere else you can.

Step 7 ~ Team Up

Join Me ~ Start making relationships with people you feel would make a good match with your business. Be of service first and come from a genuine place. When the opportunity arises, which it will, by either your creation or the universe, take that opportunity to team up to boost the business of everyone involved.

Promote Me ~ Set up an affiliate program to make it easy for happy customers, joint venture partners and other marketers to promote you with the extra incentive to be generously rewarded for their efforts. You can also be an affiliate for others and increase your profits too. While this book is about building your credibility it never helps to pay it forward to deserving businesses just like yours.

Wow that is a lot of things to do but the best part is you don't have to do them all at once to get instant credibility. Work through them bit by bit and see the results you get.

"The Power Of Building a Solid Personal Brand" ~ Katrina Kavvalos

After looking back over the past 8 years of my life, it truly dawned on me just how much I had in fact learnt, though more importantly, how much I had *grown* as a person.

Many of us go through life wondering *when* we will 'get our lucky break' and *why* reaching our goals is taking so long.

I used to hear people use the saying, 'overnight success, 10 years in the making' and I used to think to myself... *really, is that normal length of time it usually takes for one to realize their dream/goal*? It was only though my many years of struggle and frustration, that I soon realized that the answer to my question, was   YES!

Don't get me wrong, there are most definitely cases of where success for people came in just a short couple of years, but in more cases than not, reaching your desired success usually comes after you have made plenty of mistakes, have pushed through your comfort zone, which in turn forces you to learn and grow into the person you *need to become*, in order to fulfill that desired role.

It has been 8 years since I 'officially' decided that I wanted to become an entrepreneur, inspire others to pursue their dreams and to make an impact on the world, ultimately leaving behind a legacy. What I thought at the time to be a very easy task, turned out to be many years worth of learning, failures, mixed amongst the victorious moments.

It was the year 2006, where I clearly remember the morning when I was sitting in my car, driving to work thinking, *there has to be a better life than this*. I yearned for a life where I was able to be my own boss and work in the comfort of my own home, giving me the freedom and flexibility to spend more time with my husband and children.

What I didn't know all those years ago was the power of the Law of Attraction and manifesting. After having these thoughts in my head, it wasn't before long where I heard an ad on the radio, about a transformational event, called 'Unleash The Power Within', presented by Tony Robbins.

I remembered reading about Tony Robbins in a magazine article several years prior, and immediately became intrigued. After hearing the radio ad, I couldn't wait to get to work and call the number to find out more details.

When I called, I was told that the cost of the entry level into the event was $1,297.00. I almost had a heart attack because it was a lot of money to be spent on an event. I went home that afternoon and told my husband that I wanted to attend the event.

As you can imagine, he sat there quietly listening to me talk about the event, up until he heard the price, where he turned and said "I'm not paying that kind of money for someone to stand on stage and tell you how to change your life, I can do that for free." My husband thought it was a scam and wanted nothing to do with it.

To cut a very long story short, I won a ticket. Winning the ticket was a huge eye opener for me, as what *really* can be achieved in life, when you have great *desire.*

I can honestly say that this event 'UPW', literally transformed my life, as I knew it. After successfully completing four full days, including walking on fire, I was 'released' out into the real world, where I had family and friends see the new transformed me, though instead of them embracing the new me, they thought that in order for me to have changed so much within 4 days, I must have joined a cult and had been brain washed.

Tony Robbins mentions at his event that this is a quite common thing to happen, so I was prepared. I learnt to not listen to what they were saying because in my heart of hearts, I KNEW that my life would never be the same again, even though I didn't know what lay on the road ahead of me.

I attended UPW again in 2008. I wanted to attend again because I had given birth to my third child and felt as though my career had literally stopped for me, so I needed an 'inner jolt' to help me to stay motivated and on my journey. The difference with going again in 2008, than attending in 2006, was that I knew what to expect. I had a whole list of goals that I wanted to achieve from attending the four days. One major goal that I had written down was to get over my fear of public speaking. In order to do this, I knew that I had to sit right at the front, in Tony's vision and put up my hand every time Tony asked a question.

If you have ever been to a Tony Robbins event, you will notice that he makes you stand up when answering a question, so you can just imagine my fear of having to stand up in front of four thousand people. BUT, I knew I had to do it, after all, I did tell Tony that one day I will be speaking on stages, just like him, so I bit the bullet and put my hand up every time a question was asked. It was quite funny that Tony picked me to answer the questions all the time and I was soon nicknamed, the 'Mic Girl' because I was always on the microphone.

This experience truly helped me overcome my fear of public speaking. To be honest, I actually thoroughly enjoyed the experience.

I had a fear of public speaking, because I was very shy as a child and I NEVER spoke my mind, as I feared being wrong and the ridicule that came from that. I was a totally different character to the person I am today.

Today, I am a very strong, driven, talkative and friendly individual, who thoroughly enjoys networking and sincerely LOVES people. A transformation that took many years of me stepping outside my comfort zone.

Even though I had seen lots of transformations in my life, the one thing that I was still striving to figure out was my purpose. What career path I was 'supposed' to be taking?

As I wanted to have the flexibility and freedom from working from home and being my own boss. I knew that Internet Marketing sounded as a great option. I purchased as many Internet Marketing courses as I was able to and furthered my knowledge.

Back in 2009, an Internet Marketing course in which I purchased was heavily focused on Twitter. Twitter was new at that stage and not many people had heard of it, nor knew how to use it. Though this one particular teacher was focusing so much on Twitter that I knew I had to get on board.

This is where things were about to change ....

I immersed myself into Twitter so much so, that I was spending around 12-15hours a day on the platform, building and growing my connections. Before I knew it, I had almost 35,000 followers within a six month period. Many of my followers are celebrities, thought leaders and high profile people.

Due to my high Twitter following, many doors opened for me. I was offered by a US publishing company, to be a contributing author in one of their books called 'The Relationship Age', which profiled the 'world's top 20 social media experts'. This book became #1 on Amazon and therefore I was immediately propelled to #1 Best-selling author status.

Out of this experience, I had so many people asking me to help them with their social media and their personal branding that my Social Media business literally started by pure chance.

I was teaching social media and personal branding to entrepreneurs, small business owners, celebrities etc for years and loved it, though I had reached a point back in 2012, where teaching social media to others, did not 'ignite my fire' as it once did. I still loved social media, though I knew that it was time for a change. It was time to rebrand and find something that I *was* passionate   about.

I remember speaking to a dear friend of mine, who I had met on twitter. I talked about not knowing where my life was heading and feeling confused as to what I am 'supposed' to be doing with my life. At that point in time, I honestly thought that every individual was supposed to know what their purpose is and what drives them. It wasn't until later on in time **that I learnt from many successful people, that you basically DO what makes your heart sing each and every day and you will be drawn towards your destiny.**

I honestly felt as though I had reached a VERY dark moment in my life. I felt lost. My friend told me to take some time off work to 'find myself', so I did. I planned to take 3 months off work, doing absolutely nothing but waking up each day and spending time with ME.

Each and every morning when I would awake, I felt as though I had lost my mojo. I was becoming even more depressed as time went on, though something happened towards the end of those three months. I woke up one day and went into my home office. I just sat in my chair and starred at the walls. I starred and starred until I noticed my vision board, which was on the wall directly in front of my office chair.

I starred at it and realized that it needed updating, so I gathered together as many magazines as I could find in my house. I started cutting out all the pictures and words that I resonated with me. I also went online and searched for images that I couldn't find in the magazines.

After spending a full two days on my vision board, I had finished. I sat in my office chair once again, and starred at my new completed vision board wall. This time felt different. As I was looking at each individual picture and words on my vision board, I realized that 90% of the pictures that were on my vision board wall were based around the TV/Entertainment industry.

I became confused... "Why did I subconsciously cut out all these pictures", I thought. The more I was looking at them, the more perplexed I became. Then, I sat and really thought for a minute. I suddenly realized that by doing my vision board, it helped to tap into parts of my unconscious brain, and reveal inner desires that I wasn't conscious about.

I then realized that I wasn't doing anything to do with TV or the Entertainment industry. I had to decide whether to continue teaching social media, OR take a leap of faith and enter into an industry I knew NOTHING about.

There were so many things going through my head. Not having any experience was definitely a major factor, but *age* completely overrode that factor. I felt as though I was too old for the industry as I had just turned 38.

After hours of deliberating, I decided to take the plunge, and just go for it. I knew that I had nothing to lose and everything to gain, and the worst thing that could happen, was that I had a whole heap of fun trying. I had absolutely NO idea WHAT I wanted to do in the TV/Entertainment industry. I just knew that I belonged in it.

A surge of excitement had hit me and within a few hours I had found myself an agent. As I had no idea what I should be focusing, it dawned on me that I could probably become an actress, so I enrolled into every acting course I could find and started doing my research on the people in the industry that I wanted to connect with.

Once I had finished my research, I used my social media expertise to connect with influential people within the industry. One thing that I learn early on in my career was the importance of building relationships. Building relationships has been a major contributing factor to my success.

Within a few days of deciding to pursue the TV/Entertainment industry, I had been booked for commercials, photos shoots and TV appearances. All these opportunities were made possible, from using and implementing my social media expertise and *making* things happen. The POWER of social media became more apparent as time went by, as I realized that all the work that 'I' had found for myself was not through any agent.

After having attended several acting courses, it soon became apparent that learning lines every night was not something that I particularly enjoyed. Nevertheless, I kept registering for as many courses as I possibly could, to further my knowledge.

It was another usual day, where I would receive emails of all the acting courses available, where I came across this one particular email, about a course which taught all about catapulting your acting career.

Little did I know at that time, that this course would literally change the direction of life as I knew it. The event taught how to produce and direct your own film, have 'A' list actors star in it, and also create a character for yourself to be in the film. That was all good and well if you already had script idea, but I didn't. I didn't even want to come up with a script idea because it didn't feel as though it was my calling. Even though I had learnt so many things at that event, I felt as though I was back at square one.

I left the event and hurried back home because I had a christening to attend. I went to the christening and didn't get home until quite late. Before going to bed, I actually thought of the day that I had.

Without realizing, I woke up at 3am the following morning with a head full of amazing concepts for a TV show.

I couldn't contain my excitement and was unable to fall asleep again. As morning approached, I waited until an 'appropriate' time to contact the producer who had conducted the event the day prior. After mentioning my idea to him, he loved it and was excited to help me bring my idea into fruition. The idea for a TV show that I came up with REALLY FELT right, ever fiber in my body was excited and after hearing the producer's excitement, I knew that I was onto a winner.

We began at once putting the wheels into motion. TV show name, logo, etc. Even though there were definite times of stress and frustration, I kept going. Just the fact that I had someone by my side, helping along the process, put me at ease.

One and a half years into the project, I was getting closer than ever. I woke up one morning really missing teaching social media, though I actually felt as though I had a yearning to use my social media skills in the TV industry. I thought that doing the social media for The Voice Australia would be quite fun.

As I knew that I was an amazing manifestor, I put it out to the universe to deliver. The thing is, I didn't realize just how soon the universe would actually deliver. A few hours after deciding that I wanted to do the social media for a TV show, I was compelled to go visit The Voice Australia website. Low and behold, there was an advertisement about a contest, where the general public had a chance to be a VIP Social Reporter for Team Vodafone, where you could represent any coach of your choice. The competition was due to close the following day. How freaky, I thought.

I was left sitting in my chair quite perplexed. I looked at my calendar for the next day, and saw that it was filled with appointments and I literally only had one hour in which I could focus on this competition.

I didn't sleep at all that night, trying to think of what type of photo I would take and upload. I wanted the photo to clearly depict my character and one that truly showed off my creativity.

That morning I woke up and knew what I had to do. As Vodafone was the sponsor of the competition, I decided to go to a Vodafone store in a shopping centre and gather as many people together to take a photo with me in it, while holding a microphone.

I rang a girlfriend of mine to be the 'photographer' for the hour. I thought it was going to be simple. Gathering people together to take a photo with you was one thing, making sure they stayed while I continued to gather more people, was another issue.

Withstanding all the obstacles, I pulled it off. I gathered around 15 people and took the photo. I uploaded the photos along with writing in under 25 words or less 'why' I deserved to win. All within an hour.

I had selected to be Will.i.am's VIP Social Reporter, as he really inspires me, not only as an artist, but an entrepreneur and philanthropist. I began at once, doing as much research as I could about Will.i.am and started connecting with him on Twitter. The more I learnt about him, the more I was in awe with his brilliant mind and heart of gold. It wasn't before long that Will.i.am followed me back on Twitter. Now that was definitely a moment in time where I did the biggest happy dance EVER. What an absolute honor.

Will.i.am has over 12 million followers and is only following 900 or so people and 'I' was one of those 900 people. It proved to me more than ever, how important building relationships truly is.

It doesn't matter who you are trying to connect with, whether they are a celebrity, a thought leader or merely someone of influence, you have to treat them the same way you would your dear friend. Get to know them and start building a relationship with them. Make sure you are genuine about wanting to get to know someone better and sincerely take an interest in what they are doing in their business and life. GIVE as much to them as possible, WITHOUT expecting anything in return.

I won the competition, where I was to post all the behind the scenes of the show, be Will.i.am's VIP Social Reporter, for Team

Will & Team Vodafone, for The Voice Australia.

I was also privileged to have been given full access of the behind the scenes of The Voice Australia, where I was able to witness how a show on such a magnitude is put together. I also got to have a go at using the autocue. It truly felt like super star treatment, as we had our hair and makeup done on the grand final day, by the crew of professionals, so that we were able to attend the red carpet all glammed up.

I can honestly say it was one of the best experiences of my life. Not only was I able to meet and connect with the contestants and all of the coaches (Will.i.am, Joel Madden, Ricky Martin and Kylie Minogue), I felt truly blessed to have been given the opportunity to chat with and get to know one of the most influential, remarkable, talented and intelligent individuals on the planet, the man himself, Mr. Will.i.am.

The Voice experience is over and I continue working on my TV show, where my aim is to prove that no matter your age, your experience or expertise, ANYTHING is possible if you have the drive and desire, combined with taking massive action towards the goal daily.

When I look back at my journey so far, I realized that all my success and achievements to date purely stemmed from having built a solid personal brand. I have reached a point in my career, where I know how to use social media to connect with whomever I want to, though most importantly, what I excel at, is the ability to build solid relationships with people both online, as well as offline.

It is through my many years of experience and expertise, that I have been able to teach my clients how they too can successfully grow their profile, by super charging their personal brand, allowing them to stand out in their industry and to become what I call, a 'celebrity' in their industry.

You may be thinking that you are not experienced enough, or

don't have enough knowledge, but I am here to tell you that no matter where you are right now, ANYTHING is possible, but first, you must build your brand.

Once you do this, many doors will start to open, which will provide you with many great opportunities.

Katrina Kavvalos is known as the 'Queen of Marketing and Branding'. She is a #1 Best-selling Author, **VIP Social Media Reporter for artist Will.i.am & 'The Voice Australia'** and is also a Personal Branding & Social Media expert and trainer, who has built high credibility in the Social Media and Online Marketing fields.

Her high level of excellence, combined with her drive and zest for life, has contributed to her ranking in the top 1% in the world for influence and top 5% for the most viewed profile on LinkedIn.

Katrina is also ranked in the top 100 in Sydney, for most followed on Twitter and is ranked in the top 50,000 most followed globally. Katrina is followed by a large number of celebrities and thought leaders.

Katrina helps celebrities, entrepreneurs, small business owners, speakers, coaches, authors and actors, learn how to grow their profile by super charging their personal brand, allowing them to become 'celebrities' within their industry.

Katrina resides in Sydney with her husband John and three children.

Download free ebook
"5 PROVEN Ways To SUPERCHARGE Your Profile"
http://www.SuperchargeYourProfile.com

Website: http://www.KatrinaKavvalos.com

Keep Your Eyes On The Goal

Florence Chadwick was on her way to becoming the first woman to swim the Catalina Channel on July 4th, 1952. Florence had already conquered the English Channel and now with the world watching she was about set a new record. Fighting through dense fog, bone-chilling cold and sometimes sharks, she was close to achieving her goal. The weather had worsened that day and every time Florence looked through her goggles for the shore all she could see was more fog. Unable to see the shore and feeling like she was going nowhere, she gave up. Florence was extremely disappointed when she discovered that she was only half a mile from shore. She quit not because she was a quitter but because her goal was not in sight. "I'm not making excuses," Florence said, "If only I had seen the shore, I could have made it." Two months later despite bad weather she not only completed the Catalina Channel swim but she beat the men's record by two hours.

Keep your goals in sight to achieve great success!

Final Thoughts

Have fun with your business. It is hard not to fall into feeling that your business is all about pleasing other people and paying the bills. Take time to remember your big 'WHY'. The reason you started your business, what your business can provide in your life and the difference you can make in the world.

Be Enthusiastic

"Nothing great is ever achieved without enthusiasm" ~
Ralph Waldo Emerson

Many years ago, Charles Schwab was earning a salary of a million dollars a year. He was asked if his exceptional ability to produce steel was why he was being paid such a high salary. Charles Schwab replied, "I consider my ability to arouse enthusiasm among the men, the greatest asset I possess, and the way to develop the best that is in a man is by appreciation and encouragement."

Enthusiasm and desire are what change mediocrity to excellence.

A difference of only one degree in temperature turns water into steam and steam can move some of the biggest engines in the   world.

That is what enthusiasm helps us to do in our lives.

"My key to success or my success equation is pretty simple. If what you're doing's working, it's the right way. If it's not working, then it's the wrong way. Simple as that."
~ Justin Herald

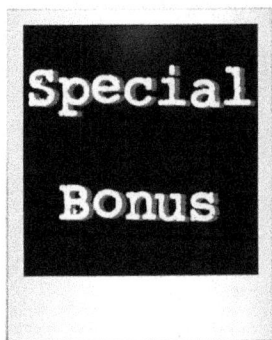

Special Bonus

I have some special bonuses for you so that you can get most or of this book.

Simply visit http://www.InstantCredibility.net

Bonus #1 ~ I.N.S.T.A.N.T. Credibility Formula™ eBook

Variety is the key to life. Now you don't have to settle for just one way to read the I.N.S.T.A.N.T. Credibility Formula™. You will now be able to read it in electronic form with an eBook copy for you to download.

Valued @ $17

Bonus #2 ~ I.N.S.T.A.N.T. Credibility Formula™ eWorkbook

I.N.S.T.A.N.T. Credibility Formula™ is full of interesting and useful exercises so you can implement what you learn. To help you work through these exercises you will receive an eWorkbook so you can print it out or save it on your computer at your leisure. A special gift to help you succeed.

Valued @ $17

Bonus #3 ~ I.N.S.T.A.N.T. Credibility Formula™ Audio Book

Now you have take the hard work out of reading and have the author read the book to you. This is ideal for busy people who want to listen while you carry out your daily tasks.

Valued @ $37

About the Author

Bored by your brand? Unleash your inner superhero to create kick ass marketing!

In a world of boring, bland, lifeless marketing and branding there lives an undiscovered hero… YOU! Here you are, competing in the jungles of suburbia for the attention of your potential clients, instead of donning your superhero cape and soaring high above your competitors.

Never Fear, Help Is On It's Way…

To show you how to UNLOCK your superhero personality, BRIGHTEN your brand to SOAR above the competition.

Starting and running a business can be an overwhelming experience. The journey is filled with so called "experts" telling you what you should do and that "their" way is the best. They look perfect, make the process sound easy and charge you a fortune to have you create another clone of THEIR business.

It's only natural that in the process you wind up feeling lost, insecure, broke and defeated.

The sad part about this is: you are SPECTACULAR!!! You know that you can really help people. You know you have what it takes to make your business work!

- The problem is… you don't look half as glamorous as these experts
- You hate to see your picture plastered all over your marketing
- You feel uncomfortable tooting your own horn
- You have lost your voice and personality, because you've blindly regurgitated someone else's idea of what your business should be about

NOW IS THE TIME TO TAKE CONTROL AND ADD CHARACTER TO YOUR BRAND!!!

Let me introduce myself. My name is Amanda Robins

I have walked in your shoes and I know exactly how it feels to know what it is like to be so good at what you do and have so much to offer but you are lost trying to create a professional appearance that you "think" everyone wants.

For the past 10 years I have has started, built and sold several businesses. I went into each wanting to make money and trying to find the expert who would teach me how to make it successful. The problem however was the more I listened to the experts the more I lost myself and my passion for my business.

That was until I started listening to my clients. They kept telling me that my marketing and what I actually did for them was so different. That they got so much more from working with me that my boring, run of the mill, basically "Blah" branding was doing my business an injustice.

Here was the big question? How do I create a brand that I am proud of, excited to share and relates to my peeps without locking myself into just one thing for the rest of my business life? (I love variety)

Faced with this information I decided to bust out of the box and "Brainstorm" was born. An idea genie on a mission to help business owners just like you discover their superpowers to reveal the true character that will help you conquer your fears, smash through obstacles and leap your way to success!

So I have recruited an extraordinary team of talented sidekicks to plot, plan and execute the heavy lifting to bring the **POW** to your branding while you fight the good fight for your clients.

Now is the time for you to join the alliance of business owners stepping up to add some oomph to their business and hear their client's call for help. Only you can solve their problems with your amazing abilities and powerful personality!

To take the first step on your journey to Superfy your brand!

NOW Is time to…

"Uncover the Superhero In YOU"

Discover the 17 POWerful reasons why you're already a superhero!

It will soon be revealed just how SPECTACTULAR you are and how you can harness your powers to add more OOMPH to your marketing and branding!

Before you know it you will be strapping on your cape, leaving your competition in the DUST!

Can you feel your power surging already?

YES!

Marvelous!

Let's take the first step…

Simply visit **www.SuperfyHQ.com** to get your free copy of "Uncover the Superhero In YOU"

Start unleashing some kick ass marketing TODAY!!!

Amanda Robins Bio

Amanda Robins is the go-to creative branding and marketing strategist for business owners and professionals who think outside the box and are looking to add personality to their boring branding.

Whether it's revealing your inner superhero, naming your signature system, birthing your credibility book or opening your awareness to the possibilities to profit from being your spectacular self or just a simple confidence boost, Amanda will help you create an authentic business presence you will feel excited, proud and confident to go out and share with the world even if they don't feel like an expert.

Amanda has a genuine interest and passion to see her clients thrive in all aspects of their life. Using her experience, stories, intuition and kick-ass listening skills, Amanda has an uncanny knack of knowing exactly what questions to ask to allow creative solutions to come to light during brainstorming sessions.

Happy to openly share her years of knowledge as a marketer, international best selling Amazon author, business owner, entrepreneur, trainer, coach, speaker, loving mother and superhero, Amanda's clients are able to get their questions answered with the reassurance that the advice given is backed by experience.

If you are passionate, focused and energetic heartcentred business owner or entrepreneur now is the time for you to connect with your authentic self, unleash your inner superhero, spread your wings and THRIVE!

For more tips on adding character to your brand go to www.AmandaRobins.com

"Now spread your wings and THRIVE!"

~Amanda Robins

InstantCredibility.com.au